PRACTICING THE SACRED ART OF LISTENING

A Guide to Enrich Your Relationships and Kindle Your Spiritual Life— The Listening Center Workshop

Kay Lindahl
FOUNDER OF THE LISTENING CENTER

Illustrations by **Amy Schnapper**

Walking Together, Finding the Way
SKYLIGHT PATHS Publishing

Practicing the Sacred Art of Listening:
A Guide to Enrich Your Relationships and Kindle Your Spiritual Life—The Listening Center Workshop

2016 Quality Paperback Edition

Library of Congress Cataloging-in-Publication Data
Lindahl, Kay, 1938–
Practicing the sacred art of listening : a guide to enrich your relationships and kindle your spiritual life—the Listening Center workshop / Kay Lindahl ; illustrations by Amy Schnapper.
    p.   cm.
ISBN-13: 978-1-893361-85-0 (pbk.)
ISBN-10: 1-893361-85-3 (pbk.)
1. Spiritual life. 2. Listening—Religious aspects. I. Title.
BL629.5.L57 L56 2003
204'.46—dc22
                                                                                2003015230

ISBN 978-1-59473-458-8 (eBook)

Manufactured in the United States of America
Cover Art: Amy Schnapper
Cover Design: Bridgett Taylor

> SkyLight Paths Publishing is creating a place where people of different spiritual traditions come together for challenge and inspiration, a place where we can help each other understand the mystery that lies at the heart of our existence.
> SkyLight Paths sees both believers and seekers as a community that increasingly transcends traditional boundaries of religion and denomination—people wanting to learn from each other, *walking together, finding the way.*

SkyLight Paths, "Walking Together, Finding the Way" and colophon are trademarks of LongHill Partners, Inc., registered in the U.S. Patent and Trademark Office.

Walking Together, Finding the Way
Published by SkyLight Paths Publishing
An Imprint of Turner Publishing Company
4507 Charlotte Avenue, Suite 100
Nashville, TN 37209
Tel: (615) 255-2665
www.skylightpaths.com

PRACTICING THE SACRED ART OF LISTENING

This book is dedicated
to my global family,
with the awareness that we are all
members of one family,
the human family.

CONTENTS

CONTENTS

Introduction

We live in a time of change and shifting paradigms. It's not always easy for us to see past the chaos with all the potential flash points for violence in the world. We wonder whether what we do as individuals can make a difference in the face of so many challenges. Two ways to counteract the feelings of powerlessness and hopelessness that often accompany this type of uncertainty are conversation and collective reflection. Even though we lead busy lives, with more to do than we can ever get done, we feel isolated, alone. Something's missing. We have an unspoken yearning for community, for being with others, for feeling that our lives matter. We are hungry to tell our stories in authentic conversations, only we have forgotten how to begin. The simple yet profound act of listening to each other opens the door to connection, understanding, and transformation.

My first book, *The Sacred Art of Listening: Forty Reflections for Cultivating a Spiritual Practice* (SkyLight Paths Publishing), introduced concepts of listening by using reflections, each one opening up a new dimension of listening. This book builds on those reflections and offers a more practical approach, with exercises and specific practices to enhance our capacity to listen. It is designed to open up our hearts to listening as a sacred art. It incorporates content from my workshops, as well as lessons learned from participants over the years.

Whenever I am asked about my background and interest in listening, the first thought that comes to mind is "It's a result of my lifetime experience." It seems as if everything I've ever done has been training me for what I'm doing now. In 1991, I began a daily spiritual practice of silent prayer and meditation. In that silence I learned about listening to God, taking the time to be silent, and listening for the wisdom in silence.

A few months later, I found myself involved in creating an interfaith organization, the Alliance for Spiritual Community. We discovered that we really wanted to spend time together learning about each other and our various belief systems. We quickly developed guidelines for practicing the art of dialogue. Learning how to listen to each other became a key component of these dialogues.

In 1997, my spiritual mentor, who was aware of my daily practice of silence and my work with dialogue, invited me to co-lead a workshop on prayer with him. As we started planning it, I could see the ways in which silent prayer was listening to God and dialogue was listening to others. Somehow I knew there was one more piece to listening. That's when I began to practice reflection, listening to my inner voice. With my mentor's nudging, I entered a discernment process about what was next for me. Out of that I realized this is the work I am called to do now. It is a gift and a blessing beyond anything I could have imagined.

This was the beginning of The Listening Center, which is the name of my company, not a physical space. Wherever I work is The Listening Center, a space and time in which we focus on listening. Actually, each of us is a center for listening—it is from our centers that we learn to listen and practice this sacred art.

Connecting with the sacred in daily life leads to a sense of inner peace, even in the midst of chaos. We experience a wholeness that transcends our differences. We find ourselves in community, with feelings of gratitude and growing compassion for others.

When we talk to each other about our fears and dreams, we open up the space for hope. When we learn how to listen to ideas that conflict with our own without becoming defensive, our hearts begin to open and we start to see each other as part of one human family. We connect at a deep level. When we practice the sacred art of listening, we also learn the art of conversation. It is this type of conversation that can transform our world.

1

What Is Listening?

Are you listening, are you really listening? The answer to this question is usually yes—since asking the question automatically causes us to pay attention, to listen up. In thinking about it, though, we might also respond by saying it all depends what you mean by listening. Am I hearing the words? Am I understanding what I hear? Am I relating to what I hear? There are any number of ways to regard listening. It's a skill that we take for granted. Of course we all listen to each other, but what do we mean when we say that? Many times we think that if we are not speaking we must be listening. It becomes part of our vocabulary of opposites: hot/cold, wet/dry, light/dark, listening/speaking.

However, something very interesting happens when people find out that I write, teach, and facilitate workshops on listening, that the name of my company is The Listening Center, or that I am the author of *The Sacred Art of Listening*. One of the first things they say is "That's wonderful! We could all learn to listen better." This is quickly followed by:

"Would you talk to my husband/wife/boss/kids/partner/sister/brother?" It seems we all know someone whom we'd like to listen to us better.

If this is true, that none of us feels other people listen to us in the way we'd like, what we are really saying is that no one is listening well, including ourselves! In that case, each of us really does need to learn how to listen better—affirming the initial reaction to my work. How can we become more effective listeners? What are we looking for when we want to be listened to? There are no simple answers to these questions, but we can explore some ideas that are designed to:

Create a new awareness of the importance of listening
Lead to more clarity about listening
Give us some practices to try out

Think of the difference it would make if each of us really felt listened to when we spoke. Imagine the time it would save to be heard the first time around, instead of having to repeat ourselves over and over again. Envision a conversation in which each person is listened to with respect, even those whose views are different from ours. This is all possible in conversations of the heart, when we practice the sacred art of listening. It takes intention and commitment. We need to slow down to expand our awareness of the possibilities of deep listening. The simple act of listening to each other can transform all of our relationships. Indeed, it can transform the world, as we practice being the change we wish to see in the world.

"When people talk, listen completely.... Most people never listen."[1] There are some interesting statistics that validate this claim by Ernest Hemingway. Most of us spend about 45 percent of our waking hours listening, yet we are distracted, preoccupied, or forgetful about 75 percent of that time. Marketing studies indicate that the average attention span for adults is 22 seconds. (Think about television commercials, which usually last 15 to 30 seconds.) When someone has finished speaking, we remember about half of what we heard. Within a few hours we can recall only about 20 percent. The number of adults who have had any training in listening skills is less than 5 percent of our population. It hasn't been part of the curriculum in most schools.

After hearing these statistics, a business executive reflected: "This is very interesting. I just realized that I spend a great deal of time preparing myself to speak. I don't think I have ever prepared myself to listen." Deep listening is a forgotten art.

Our families provide us with our first experiences in listening. Each of us has a certain style of listening based on our childhood environment. As we grew older and entered school, we discovered more sophisticated ways to communicate and developed additional styles of listening. Relationships with our peers added new habits and patterns. Unless we are part of the 5 percent who have had formal training in listening, we continue to pick up our skills from our surroundings, which may or may not be conducive to effective listening.

We are inundated with examples of poor listening in movies and on television. People are constantly interrupting each other. Shouting is used as a way to make a point or to convince someone to do something. Often the one who is supposedly listening to another person is actually working on the computer, writing a report, or engaged in some other activity. Resolving differences frequently involves physical or verbal violence. There are very few examples of peacemaking solutions. The use of sarcasm, humiliation, and put-downs is rampant. We are being educated in our communication skills by mass media. Learning how to listen well is left to us to discover on our own.

Another factor that adds to the importance of listening is that we live in a country with enormous cultural and religious diversity. Diversity provides us with one of the major challenges and opportunities of our time. We've become a laboratory for the world. If we can learn to live together in harmony in this country, it can be done anywhere. This calls for a way of listening that transcends words and belief systems. Learning to truly listen to one another is the beginning of new understanding and compassion, which deepens and broadens our sense of community. Listening is the first step in making people feel valued.

What is listening? There are many definitions—and we each have our own based on our personalities, backgrounds, and training. This book considers three ways to define listening, and each one is more of a way to think about listening than the "right" answer.

The first assertion about listening is that it's a choice. Choosing to listen to someone else is a decision. Most of the time we are completely unaware that we are making a choice. Have you ever had the experience of listening to someone and all of a sudden you realize that you haven't heard a word for the past minute or so? Your attention is no longer with the other person. You have unconsciously chosen not to listen.

It's easier to notice conscious choices. If we don't want to hear what someone is saying, we can tune him or her out in an instant. Sometimes it's because we are uncomfortable with the topic, or we are simply not interested in it. Sometimes we know that we should listen but we worry that if we really listen we might just have to change something about the way we think or the way we lead our lives. Or we may hear a person's words, but we're not really there—something in our own minds has become more important.

Most likely, we've all been on the other side of this, too, when we are speaking and other people tune us out. They are still physically present and may even look as if they are listening. We just sense that they have left us and are no longer paying attention to what we are saying. We keep talking and are relieved when they tune in again.

Listening is not a passive activity. It's not about being quiet or even hearing the words. It is an action, and it takes energy to listen. The first time I became aware of the energy factor was at an international gathering, where I was part of a small group of eight people. We were from four different continents, spoke four different languages, and worshiped in four different faith traditions. Our task was to make recommendations for one part of a document we were creating as a large body. For two days, I went to bed exhausted. I couldn't imagine why I was so tired because I was getting enough sleep and had not been physically active. All we had been doing was sitting around talking and listening. Then it occurred to me that it took a lot of energy to listen with such intention. I was acutely aware of each person as he or she spoke and was committed to understanding each contribution. It was quite a workout!

Once we become aware of listening as a choice, we will notice that we have many opportunities to practice choosing to listen in our daily lives. It is a profound awakening.

The second way to define listening is that it is a gift—in fact, one of the greatest gifts we can give another is to listen to her or him with total attention. Think about a time when someone was truly listening to you—not figuring out what to say next, wishing you would hurry up so she or he could speak, or mentally reviewing a to-do list. The person was simply there, listening to you. You felt understood, refreshed, whole, connected, healed. It's what we are looking for when we express our desire to be listened to. What a rare occurrence in this fast-paced, information-based culture of the twenty-first century!

You might also have had the experience of people thanking you for all the help you gave them at a particular point in their lives—and you're wondering what they're talking about because you can't remember doing anything. You had simply given them the gift of listening. Thinking about listening as a gift that you either give or receive places a new emphasis on the value of listening. It makes it easier to slow down and savor the conversation, either by opening up to receive the gift or by extending the hospitality of giving the gift.

A few years ago, a member of my family was going through a difficult time. My response was to check in once a week with a phone call. After I said hello, I spent the rest of the time listening. This went on for about six months. I didn't give it any further thought. Just recently this family member brought it up by telling me how much it meant that I had called every week, and how helpful it had been. I hadn't given advice, lectured, or offered resources. I just listened. Journalist and author Paul Hawken adds this wisdom: "When we listen to people our own language softens. Listening may be the cardinal act of giving.... I think it is the source of peace."[2]

Third, listening is an art. When we think of describing something as an art we may think of music, painting, dance, drama, poetry, drawing, photography, or architecture, to name a few. We also describe some experiences or actions as art, such as the art of teaching, the art of medicine, the art of counseling, the art of preaching, the art of coaching. What do we mean when we say that? I don't think we are referring to the technique involved. We are talking about that extra something, something special that elevates the experience or act to an art. It happens with listening, too.

There are many wonderful tools and techniques for more effective listening, such as active listening, empathic listening, relational listening, and body language. The premise of my work is that listening is more than technique. When two people are deeply listening to one another, we sense that not only are they present to each other, but they also are present to something beyond their individual selves—some call it spiritual, holy, or sacred. Musicians refer to it as aesthetic rapture, mystics describe it as ecstasy, athletes call it being in the zone, and jazz artists say they are in the groove. All of them speak about it as a moment when time stands still. They are simply being in the experience. It is the same with listening.

Being truly listened to is one of those experiences that we cannot observe in the moment. We can only describe it afterward. When we are in it, that's all there is. A friend told me about his encounter with a storeowner as he was shopping for a wedding gift. The elderly gentleman began to tell my friend a story about the time he was in a concentration camp during World War II. My friend listened, first in polite interest, then in fascination and appreciation until he got caught up in the moment. He described it as being taken to another world. Nothing else mattered. Other people in the store, whatever was going on outside—he was no longer aware of them. There was a tremendous connection between the two men, and my friend left feeling he had been blessed by the listening. He said it had been an honor to listen.

For years, as I was raising my family, it seemed as though I was the one doing all the listening. After my children grew up and left home, I found myself lonely. I can still remember the first time someone really listened to me. I felt as though that person was there just for me. I could share from my soul. I didn't have to censor what I said. It was healing and nurturing. There was a great sense of connection. The fountain of my being had been replenished. It brought me peace beyond understanding.

The listener is also nourished by these exchanges. Not only is there the connection, but there also is a sense of opening to something new. As the other person is sharing herself, speaking about the most important things in her life, the listener is also transformed. Once we begin to think about listening as a gift that we give to someone else, we often find that we open up the space for even more listening within ourselves. Our capacity to listen expands.

With the awareness of this possibility, the next question is, How do we get there? How do we access being in the zone? There are no quick and easy answers but, as with all arts, we can focus on some practices that prepare us for this experience by engaging three foundational qualities of listening: silence, reflection, and presence.

Anyone who wants to be good at something practices. Musicians, dancers, and athletes are always practicing, continuing to fine-tune their talent. Many musicians and dancers practice at least four to six hours or more each day. Those who excel in sports also spend hours every day working out. It's the practice that creates the miracles on the stage or the field or the court. It's the same with listening. We need to exercise our listening muscles, and we do that by practicing. We want to create the equivalent of muscle memory, a state when our response is automatic and we no longer have to think about it because we have practiced regularly. As we practice we begin to notice how these concepts relate to all areas of our lives. They are about being, not doing. We become a listening presence.

Listening looks easy, but it's not simple. Every head is a world.

—CUBAN PROVERB

Each of us has our own unique perspective of the world, our own worldview. We listen from that view, mostly without recognizing that we are doing so. Once we acknowledge that the way we hear something may not be what was actually said, we are on the journey to sacred listening.

As with any new skill, learning to listen takes effort, attention, and practice. The motivation to learn to listen can come in many forms. It may be in the field of relationships—at home, at school, or on the job. Perhaps you would like to have more harmony, respect, and understanding in your relationships. Or you would like more closeness with others. Perhaps you'd like to have a conversation that opens up your heart; you'd like to talk about things that are meaningful to you but you don't know how to go about it. Maybe you'd like to slow down your fast pace so you can actually be aware of life in the moment. You may be looking for a better way to manage conflicts when they occur. Or you may be interested in exploring your spiritual journey in more depth.

Once you are committed to learning more about the art of listening, you are ready to start practicing. Each conversation becomes an opportunity for practice.

Practices

The first practice is to become aware of opportunities for listening.
Notice what happens when you choose to listen.

Notice when you unconsciously choose not to listen. What happens when you come back to the conversation?

Identify someone who has given you the gift of listening. Acknowledge him or her for doing so.

Consciously choose to give someone the gift of your listening. What happened?

Recall a time when you experienced listening as an art. What happened? How did you feel?

Observe people in conversation. See whether you can identify those who practice listening as an art.

Listening is a creative force that transforms relationships. Listening to yourself elicits full self-expression—it is speaking from your soul. Listening is being fully present—to Spirit, to self, to others. Listening is a sacred act.

2

CONTEMPLATIVE LISTENING

One basic quality of the sacred art of listening is silence. Common sense tells us that there is a time for speaking and a time for silence. However, if we look at our educational process, we spend a lot of time teaching vocabulary and how to use words and very little time, if any, teaching the values of silence and listening.

We begin the practice of the sacred art of listening by exploring the quality of silence, also called contemplative listening. The original usage of the word *contemplate* meant to access a place of not knowing, of not thinking, of simply being present. Meditation was the practice of thinking—moving thoughts from the head to the heart. Our modern usage of these terms is just the opposite. If someone says, "I want to contemplate that," it is translated into "I want to think about that." If someone says, "I want to meditate," we translate that into meaning "I want to be in a place of no thought." Contemplative listening draws on the original meaning of the word and is about listening to the silence, listening beyond words. Most religious traditions acknowledge the importance of silence. The Quakers are particularly known for their practice of silence.

They talk about it as creating a space for God to work within.

You may already participate in a contemplative practice, so you will be familiar with some of its techniques and benefits. Silence is a key element of listening as a sacred art. Contemplative listening is about listening to God—exploring our relationship to Source. It's taking time to slow down and listen. We are so busy running around doing things. Contemplative listening is the practice of stopping for a moment, being quiet, learning to listen to the silence.

There's a wonderful story about Mother Teresa, who was asked what she did when she prayed to God. "Oh," she said, "that's easy. I listen." And what does God do? "Oh," she replied, "God listens." This is contemplative listening.

I'm reminded of a technique in farming in which the soil lies fallow for a season, plowed yet not planted, resting, allowing the soil to be enriched by nature so it will be more fertile ground for the next planting. It is this resting from all of our doing and all of the noise in our lives that creates rich soil for God to go to work in. It prepares us to get to know the kind of silence out of which we listen more deeply. Sister Wendy, a contemplative nun who uses her love of art to draw her into silent meditation, puts it this way: "Silence is essentially a surrender to the holiness of the divine mystery."[1]

Remember that time when someone was deeply listening to you— what it felt like to have someone really get what you were saying. It most likely inspired you to articulate your innermost thoughts and feelings, freed you to express the essence of yourself. The person who was listening to you was doing so out of a deep silence. As we practice being silent inside, we make more room for others—we have more space in which to listen. According to Meister Eckhart, a fourteenth-century Dominican mystic, "There is nothing so much like God as silence."[2]

Those of us living in twenty-first-century America are not easy with silence. Think about it for a minute. In addition to the "white noise" of our computers, appliances, copiers, traffic, and machinery, we are inundated with deliberate noise. Supermarkets, most stores, banks, and almost all public buildings have speakers blaring pop music from tapes, CDs, or radio stations. When we phone someone and are put on hold, we are subjected to music or a commercial or an infomercial. We are talked at on the Internet. People talking on cell phones and responding to pagers are common occurrences everywhere we go.

Think about the last time someone asked for a minute of silence at a public gathering. Chances are it lasted less than 15 seconds. At that point people begin to clear their throats or shuffle paper, impatient with the silence. We are uncomfortable with longer periods. Or think about a social situation where there's a buzz of people talking and suddenly there's a lull in the conversation. The room becomes quiet. It's as though this silence creates a vacuum that sucks words out of people. It doesn't really matter what is said, just as long as there is noise again. Anything to fill the void—we are addicted to noise. Brother David Steindl-Rast, a Benedictine monk and contemporary mystic, says: "Without silence there can be no listening. We need to renew our ancient friendship with silence; it is older than our flirtation with Muzak."[3]

Even places that were bastions of silence have been impacted by this discomfort. Libraries used to have a kind of reverent hush to them. Now they are often linked with coffeehouses and casual chatter and people talking on cell phones. Recently I was in a library in which pop music was blaring from speakers located throughout the room. Audiences in movie theaters, concert halls, and Broadway theaters no longer maintain a respectful silence during performances. We bring boom boxes, cell phones, and TV sets to the beach. We are so used to noise that we don't know how to react to silence. It's uncomfortable. We are suspicious of silence because it has no boundaries. It's not easy to define or control.

And yet there is a richness and a grace to silence. We could all use more time for silence, for listening. It is out of silence that we can truly listen to someone else. If we are speaking, we hear only what we already know. When we are listening, we may learn something new. Hebrew sage Solomon ibn Gabirol noted: "The beginning of wisdom is silence. The second stage is listening."

On some instinctive level we seem to know about the wisdom in silence, in spite of our discomfort with it. I suspect that some of our discomfort has to do with concerns about time. We're always in a hurry to do the next thing on our list. This poem by Nobel Peace Prize winner Mairead Corrigan Maguire offers her perspective on our need for silence.

Take time to listen to the birds,
the waves,
the wind.
Take time to breathe in the air,
the earth,
the ocean.
Take time to be still,
to be silent,
to allow God to fill you up
with deep peace and love.[4]

Silence provides time for our souls to be present. We are used to being present in our heads, our minds, our intellects. The innermost self may take a while to surface. It was said about Lao-tzu: "He listened. Such listening as this enveloped us in a silence that at last we could hear who it is we are meant to be." It is in silence that we begin to know who we are. Once we experience the stillness we become more open to compassion, love, and service.

What is contemplative listening? Slowing down, being in silence, listening to God, Source, Ultimate Being. There are many kinds of contemplative practices, each with opportunities to be silent and listen. Prayer is one form and is often thought about as a time to talk while God listens to us. However, most relationships are two-way streets—we need to listen as well as talk. According to the great Indian activist Mahatma Gandhi, "God speaks to us every day, only we don't know how to listen." Silent prayer leads us from conversation to communion.

An interesting point in the English language encourages us to think about silence and listening. Look at the six letters that spell L-I-S-T-E-N. Notice that the same six letters also spell S-I-L-E-N-T. So in this language, silence is embedded in listening.

One of my favorite books is *Gift from the Sea* by Anne Morrow Lindbergh. She was the busy mother of five children and the wife of a famous pilot. One summer she spent weeks alone at the shore. The book is a compilation of her reflections on that time.

> We seem so frightened today of being alone that we never let it happen. Even if family, friends, and movies should fail, there is still the radio or television to fill up the void. Even day-dreaming was more creative than this; it demanded something of oneself and it fed the inner life. Now, instead of planting our solitude with our own dream blossoms, we choke the space with continuous music, chatter and companionship to which we do not even listen. It is simply there to fill the vacuum. When the noise stops there is no inner music to take its place. We must re-learn to be alone."[5]

What can we do to cultivate silence and listen for that wisdom? First of all, notice how much noise there is in your life. Notice all of the external distractions. The simple task of creating this awareness can inform you of ways to incorporate silence. You might discover that you can turn off some of the noise yourself, or you can request that the volume be lowered on the piped-in music or that computers or copiers be turned off when not in use.

One of the best ways to cultivate silence is to begin a daily practice of silence. It doesn't matter what form it takes. Some people enjoy sitting and meditating, others find that walking works better. Some people lead into silence by reading, listening to music, or chanting. You might want to turn off the radio, tape player, or CD in your car. I started this last practice a couple of years ago and I truly look forward to my quiet times while driving. My car becomes a sanctuary. I enjoy the richness, inspiration, and breathing room of silence—listening beyond words. Find a minute or two each day to consciously be silent. Silence shifts from something empty, lonely, and to be avoided to something rich, filled with life, and yearned for.

Mini-retreats are another way to connect to silence. These are brief time-outs in the midst of daily life. They are a conscious way to explore your inner life, to take the time to listen to God or Spirit, to slow down enough so you can hear and acknowledge or question what God is doing in your life. A few examples are:

- Go outside or look out the window at the sky for a few minutes, and allow your mind to rest.
- Slow down to a stroll instead of power walking, to take in what you see.
- Listen attentively to music; let it wash over you.

- Read a poem. Reflect on it.
- Focus on your breath; listen to yourself breathe in and out.
- Take a 3-minute stretch break.

These mini-retreats are a way for us to regain perspective and balance the calmness and peace of our inner lives with the fast pace and sometimes chaotic nature of our outer lives.

Many people find that setting up a sacred space in their homes supports the practice of silence. It can be as simple as choosing one of the chairs in your home as your special place for silence, prayer, and meditation. Or you can set aside a corner of a room, a windowsill, a cupboard, or the top of a dresser and add sacred objects to the space. A sacred space can also be outside in your garden or on a balcony or deck. It's your space for silence, inspiration, and solace. This space becomes a reminder of the sacred and of your relationship to the Divine.

Practices

The following practices are designed to give you an experience of three different ways to access the quality of silence. The first one uses music, the second incorporates physical movement, and the third focuses on inner silence. You will gain the most benefit from these practices by spending at least 15 to 20 minutes on each one. If you have an hour, do all of them in one sitting. They also are effective if you do them individually. Once you have experienced all three, you will have a sense of the type of contemplative practice that works best for you.

PRACTICE 1 • MEDITATING WITH MUSIC

For the first practice, you will need a recording of some restful music. Chanting, harp music, and the sounds of nature work well. My favorite is Taizé music. This is a form of chanting that has been developed over the past sixty years. It comes from the Taizé community, which is in the Burgundy region of France. Founded in the 1940s by a Christian monk, Brother Roger, as a response to the devastation of World War II, Taizé is a place for ecumenical prayer and reconciliation. Three times a day, the brothers and pilgrims gather at the Church of Reconciliation and join in a single prayer. To facilitate participation by people who do not have a common language, a simple yet powerful style of singing has evolved. There are many CDs of Taizé music available. Whatever you choose, find one that has a track that lasts for at least ten minutes.

Sit in a comfortable chair. Place both feet on the floor, with your hands resting in your lap. Close your eyes. Listen to the music and begin singing along as you get used to the words and melody. Allow yourself simply to be present with the music. Let it flow over you, work through you. At the end of the chant, remain in silence for a minute as you reenter the present moment.

Most people find this a very peaceful experience. It seems to help us slow down. Even our breathing becomes more relaxed. Sometimes it can be emotional, as the beauty and peace of the music touches the soul. A woman in a recent workshop found that she couldn't relax, as the music allowed her to notice how tense she was throughout her body. She had no idea she was carrying around so much tension. It was a wake-up call to her to find ways to relax.

After your experience ask yourself these questions:

- What was this like for me? How did I feel?
- What did I notice about myself?
- What worked? What didn't work?

PRACTICE 2 • WALKING MEDITATION

Walking meditation is a physical movement. It can be done inside or outdoors. Find a place where you won't be interrupted and where you can walk in a circle without stopping. The instruction is to walk very slowly around the circle. Notice your feet when you start out. Consciously lift one foot and put it down just in front of your other foot. Shift your balance and lift up your other foot and place it just in front of the first foot. Once you get the very slow rhythm of this walking, choose a short phrase, which you will silently repeat to yourself over and over again. Examples of phrases are:

Kyrie Eleison ("Lord have mercy").
God is beautiful and loves beauty.
The peace of the Lord be always with you.
Be still and know that I am God.
Teach me your way, O God.
God is forgiving, compassionate.
Where there is forgiveness there is God.

Once you have completed your circle, stand still for a minute as you return to the present moment.

Most people find it a challenge to walk so slowly at first. It's even hard to balance the body. Once you get into the rhythm, it becomes a more contemplative experience. If you are outdoors, you may become aware of things you never noticed before—the feel of the air, or the buzzing of a small bee, or the crunch of the gravel, or the fragrance of the flowers. If you are inside you may notice things that you have taken for granted, such as the texture of the floor, the color of the wall, the detail of a picture frame. Others find that this practice helps them focus internally, and they notice their breathing, and then the meandering of their mind in relation to the phrase they use. Other people find the phrase balances their walking. Some get frustrated at the slow pace. We are so used to walking to get someplace. One man reported that he couldn't remember ever walking without a destination. He found the practice quite refreshing. Some do not like the physical aspect of this practice. Each person has a preference for a particular practice. The challenge is to find the one that works best for you.

After your experience ask yourself these questions:

- What was this like for me? How did I feel?
- What did I notice about myself?
- What worked? What didn't work?

PRACTICE 3 • CENTERING PRAYER

Henri Nouwen, a Catholic priest, introduces us to the final practice with this thought: "Prayer, therefore, is God's breathing in us…. Being useless and silent in the presence of our God belongs to the core of all prayer."[6]

Centering Prayer is an ancient method for opening up to the presence of the Divine. The practice has been known by many names over the centuries. The earliest was *monologion,* or the one-word prayer. It was used by early monks in the Christian church and carried forth in monasteries for centuries. It was revised in the twentieth century by three Roman Catholic monks: Father M. Basil Pennington, Father Thomas Keating, and Father William Menninger. They were residents at an abbey in Massachusetts at the time of the Second Vatican Council, when Catholics were advised to revere and support the work of the Spirit in other traditions. The monks decided to learn about contemplative practices and began with a Hindu teacher, Swami Satchidananda, followed by a visit to Buddhist monks nearby. They realized that Eastern contemplative practices were similar to an old Christian prayer and that it was time to share this traditional practice in a very simple and practical way. They began teaching workshops, using the phrase "going to your center" to describe the experience. The contemporary name for this prayer came from the first workshop outside the monastery, when one of the team members used the term Centering Prayer during his part of the teaching.

This is a prayer of intention—the intention to be in the presence of the Divine Presence. We open our minds and hearts to God. It's like those times when we sit with a close friend, spouse, or partner, knowing that we don't have to say anything. We can just hang out together with the intention of being with each other. No words are necessary. Nothing is expected from us.

Centering Prayer is very simple, which is sometimes hard for us to understand. We tend to equate value with complexity. Yet there's a certain elegance to the simple. We don't have to worry about doing it right. As long as we have the intention to be with God, there is no right or wrong way. There is no place to get to or any particular result to look for. There's no way to judge or analyze the experience. In fact, it's the kind of experience that we can describe only later. While we are in the moment of the experience, that's all there is.

The best posture is to sit comfortably in a chair, with both feet on the floor, hands resting on your lap, and eyes gently closed. The aim is to let the body rest deeply during the centering, wholly relaxed and supported.

1. Take a moment to quiet down. Let faith and love of God's presence be at the center of your being.

Some people find it useful to begin by taking a couple of deep breaths. Others begin by reading a devotional passage or listening to some peaceful music.

2. To dwell in this state of Presence, choose a word—a love word, a prayer word, or a sacred word, such as love, hope, grace, *abba* (father), or peace—as a symbol that expresses your intention to be with God. Gently introduce your word, supporting your consent to be in this Presence.

Take some prayerful time to choose your word. It is best to have a word with no more than 2 or 3 syllables. Use the same word throughout the sitting.

3. Whenever you become aware of anything else (thoughts, feelings, sounds, sensations), simply, gently return to the Presence with the use of your word.

Often people become aware of a noise, a body sensation, an emotion, a memory, an image, or any number of thoughts. As soon as you are conscious of any of these, reintroduce your word, gently, like a feather (not a baseball bat!). The word is not a mantra, constantly repeated. It is used only when you become aware of something. Then it leads you back to the Presence, instead of with the thought, feeling, sensation, or sound.

When you have finished, let peace flow up to the conscious levels of your being by returning slowly to the present moment, gradually opening your eyes. Sit for another minute or two before moving on to your daily routine.

The recommended time for Centering Prayer is 20 minutes, practiced twice a day. You can have a clock nearby to help you time your session. Some people set a timer. It is best to muffle the noise of the timer by putting it under a pillow or in another room. It can be jarring if a loud noise goes off while you're practicing this prayer.

You may find that you are using your word a lot, as the thoughts keep on coming. As you become more familiar with this practice, you will grow more comfortable simply letting your thoughts go, knowing that sometimes you will have lots of thoughts and other times you won't remember having many at all. Each time is different. The point is to practice every day. It's not about doing, it's about being.

After your experience ask yourself these questions:

- What was this like for me? How did I feel?
- What did I notice about myself?
- What worked? What didn't work?

Mahatma Gandhi said: "It is better in prayer to have a heart without words than words without a heart."[7]

There are many different approaches to slowing down the mind. Many people find it useful to begin with practices that gradually lead them to a contemplative place. Music, reading, and walking are a few ideas. For some it may be zoning out in front of the TV. One of the women in a recent workshop noted that her husband had to have the TV on for a while when he came home. This really bothered her, and they finally got to the root of it. He had a high-stress job, and it was hard for him to slow down when he got home. Somehow the TV did it for him. So these approaches may come in unorthodox forms!

Other types of contemplative practices include walking the labyrinth; chanting in all traditions; praying the rosary; using prayer beads; drumming; practicing breathing meditations; and gazing at a religious icon, a flame from a candle, or fire. The most important thing is to find the one that works for you. Then make an appointment with yourself and show up. We make appointments for everything else in our lives. If we really want to develop our capacity to be in silence, to grow spiritually, then we must practice regularly. There is something about the discipline of a daily practice that transforms us. In this case, it transforms our relationship to silence, our relationship to Source. It opens us up to the miracle of God's presence everywhere. We learn how to listen. We learn how to recognize God. It is a holy practice.

3

Reflective Listening

Listening involves our whole being. The Chinese incorporate several aspects of listening in the symbol that is used to depict this act. Beginning 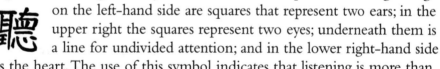 on the left-hand side are squares that represent two ears; in the upper right the squares represent two eyes; underneath them is a line for undivided attention; and in the lower right-hand side is the heart. The use of this symbol indicates that listening is more than hearing words; it encompasses our ears, eyes, undivided attention, and heart. As we practice the sacred art of listening, we are relearning this wisdom.

Listening is often thought of as something we do for someone else, outside ourselves, out in the world. Reflective listening is about listening inward, listening to our self—our True Self—getting to know the voice of our soul. In deepening our relationship with ourselves, we develop the sensitivity to listen to our inner voice. There's a wonderful poem by Sue Bender that sets the tone for this chapter.

Listening to your heart,
finding out who you are
is not simple.
It takes time for the
chatter to quiet down.
In the silence of "not doing"
we begin to know what we feel.
If we listen and hear
what is being offered,
then anything in life
can be our guide.
Listen.[1]

A few years ago I had an experience with reflection that really impacted my life. I was at a conference of about two hundred people. We had been divided into small groups of eight to work on various tasks. I became quite passionate about our group's task and was asked to be the one reporting back to the large group the next morning. I woke up with laryngitis. I could speak no louder than a whisper. Thanks to the modern technology of sensitive microphones, I was able to make my report. Some attendees told me they thought that people listened more intently because my voice was so soft. My reflection, however, taught me something else. It seems that I had to lose my voice (coming from my ego) to find the voice that I am (coming from my soul, my passion). This has become a very useful tool for me. When I remember,

I check in and ask myself who's talking. Is it my voice or the voice that I am? I would not have learned this valuable lesson without the practice of reflection.

Reflective listening is about listening for the questions. We are constantly pulled away from our innermost self and encouraged to look outward for answers instead of listening for the questions. Rilke's advice to the young poet was: "Live the questions. Perhaps then, someday far in the future, you will gradually, without ever noticing it, live your way into the answer."[2]

In our culture, we have been trained to come up with instant answers. A friend who is a teacher told me about a research project that measured the amount of time that lapsed between a classroom teacher asking a question and calling upon a student for a response. It was one second or less. The researchers suggested that the teachers wait at least seven seconds before calling on someone to see what would happen. What they discovered was that the children who hardly ever raised their hands began to do so. With that extra amount of time, they found that they did have something to say. The response from the children whose hands were normally raised before the teacher finished asking the question was also changed. It was more thoughtful and on target. With the additional six seconds, they had time to reflect, to think about what they were going to say, to probe deeper than the first thought that came to mind. We, too, can be trained to reflect before we speak.

How do we get to know this inner voice? Again, it's a practice. Take a few breaths before responding to a situation, question, or comment.

Ask yourself what wants to be said next. Not "What do I want to say?" (from the ego) but "What wants to be said?" (from the soul). Wait for your inner voice to respond. Listen for your true wisdom to reveal itself. These are not the types of questions we ordinarily ask ourselves. It may seem strange at first, and yet it's in the asking of these questions that we discover our inner voices. It's a slowing down, waiting, practicing patience.

Practices

PRACTICE 1 • THE LISTENING STICK

This practice is for small groups of no more than six people. It can be done in pairs or triads but is most effective in groups of four to six. It will:

- Give you a profound experience of deep listening—to your inner self (your soul) and to the soul of others.
- Create an awareness of listening and being listened to.
- Deepen your respect for others.
- Develop a sense of community.

One time when we did this exercise in pairs, two teenagers who were best friends were partners. They reported afterward that they were amazed at what they found out about each other. They were sure that they knew everything there was to know in a close friendship. They discovered that this conversation was at a deeper level than any they'd ever had.

Another time I was working with the customer service department of a company. The small groups were all coworkers who knew each other in a specific capacity. Some reported that the activity was a challenge at first because they felt really vulnerable accessing their inner voices in front of their professional peers. What they discovered was that the questions evoked authentic responses that were honored and appreciated by the others. In fact, they felt more heard than they ever did in their ordinary workplace.

Most groups respond that they are stunned by the bond that develops in the group in a very short time. By accessing our innermost selves, we begin to find that we can relate to each other at a deeper level. By not interrupting each other, we really begin to listen to what the other has to say. Once we do that, we connect in a very powerful way.

This practice, called the Listening Stick, is a workout designed to exercise the muscle of reflection, or listening to our inner voice, which is weak in our culture.

Find an article to use for your listening stick, such as a marker, a pencil, or any small round object. Arrange chairs in a small circle. Do not sit around a table. It can form a barrier, which gets in the way of deep listening. You will find it easier to listen to each other when you are really close together—knee to knee.

Give the listening stick to the person who will begin the exercise. As a group, choose a question that asks for a personal reflection. Examples are:

What gives you joy?
How do you respond to anger?
What are you afraid of?
Where do you go for support?
How do you nurture your spirit?

When you are ready to begin:

1. If you are the person holding the listening stick, state the question to which you will respond, but personalize it. For example, the first question above would be stated as "What gives me joy?"

2. Close your eyes and spend the next 20 to 30 seconds in silent reflection on the question.

Take your time—this is not about an instant answer. It is your opportunity to practice accessing your inner wisdom to find your personal response to the question. There is no right answer or wrong answer—in fact, there is no answer, simply your response.

3. Notice your immediate response. Go deeper. Trust your intuition. Allow your inner voice to come through.

While you are reflecting on your question, you may notice that you have an immediate response. Keep on reflecting. There is almost always something at a deeper level. Use the 20 to 30 seconds to go inside yourself. One man reported that he knew his response to the question right away. However, he decided to play the game and wait to see whether there was something else. After about 10 seconds he found that his response had altered somewhat. Again, though, after he looked at his watch, he decided to continue reflecting for the full 30 seconds. He was amazed to find himself saying things that he had barely articulated to himself at his most profound thinking times, much less to a group of mostly strangers. He said it was a transformative experience and made him realize how much he comes up with an instant response, rather than checking in to see whether there is something from a deeper level.

4. Open your eyes. Speak to your group. Say whatever comes to your mind in response to the question. Take as much time as you need to say what there is to be said.

You may notice that words come slowly or that there are pauses as you learn to listen to your inner voice. You will know when you are done. It's a sense that there is no more to say right now.

5. When you're finished, reflect again. Go back inside and ask yourself: "What's the next question that wants to be asked?" It will come to you. This is not a linear exercise, so the question may or may not relate to what you've just said. Listen for the question without thinking about who will be responding to it. Just ask the question.

When you reflect on the next question, you may find that something will come up right away. Keep reflecting to see whether there's another question behind it. There may not be, but the process of taking 20 to

30 seconds will let you know. At other times it seems as if no question comes up. Trust in the process. Even if it's just a phrase that comes to mind, speak it and see whether it doesn't turn into a question. One time a woman shared that nothing was coming to mind. Finally she decided that she'd just open her mouth and start speaking. When she did, a question came forth. This is an exercise in listening for your inner voice, for the wisdom inside. Trust in it. Allow that voice to come through.

6. Open your eyes and state the question that comes to you and pass the listening stick to the person on your left, who will respond to the new question and repeat the process. The last person to respond also generates a question, even though the exercise stops at that point.

When you're not holding the listening stick, your job is to listen to what is being said. It is not a time for you to respond to what has been said, or to ask questions. Listen for each other's souls. You may find yourself doing your own reflection during the times of silence. You might want to pray for the person who is reflecting, that he or she will connect with his or her inner voice. Notice that your response may be very different. Notice how your mind may wander when someone else is speaking. Train yourself to be present. Practice undivided attention.

Most of the time when we are in groups and each person is going to respond to the same question, it's almost impossible to listen to the person speaking because the voice inside of you is mentally preparing what you are going to say. One of the beauties of this exercise is that you don't know what question you will be responding to ahead of time, so you don't need to spend your time rehearsing your response. You are free to be fully present with the person who is speaking—to get to know the essence of another's being, to listen with your heart.

When I am teaching this exercise, I go over the guidelines and explain them much as you've just read. Then I model the exercise by asking for a question from the group. I never know what I will be asked, so I am really in the same position as each group member will be during the exercise. When I have finished and generated a new question, it becomes the first question for each circle. After that the questions change. (A sample demonstration is in the Appendix.)

When everyone has finished, acknowledge and thank one another. Spend the next 15 minutes debriefing the experience. Explore the following questions:

- What was it like for you?
- What did you hear?
- What did you notice about the process?
- What opened up for you?

One of the most common comments at the conclusion of this exercise is that each person feels so much more connected to the others in his or her small group. It is often expressed as feeling the Spirit moving in the group. Frequently, someone will say: "How did you know to ask that question? It was just the perfect one for me." People also notice that there is a thread or pattern to the questions, each one leading to a deeper place.

Participants report that, when listening, it's hard at first not to respond to what another person is saying. We are so used to offering advice or empathy or information. It's an unusual experience just to listen. By the time the second or third person has the listening stick, the others in the group find that they are fascinated to hear what the person has to say. And they use the reflection times to support the person reflecting.

A woman once revealed at the conclusion of this exercise that, as she was listening to the instructions, she thought it was out of the question that she would be able to participate. She found herself thinking, "I can't do this." She began to feel safer in her small group after the first two people had responded, so when it was her turn she was ready to try. What she noticed was that her first response to the question presented to her was off-the-cuff and superficial. As she reflected, she got in touch with her own creativity. Her comment afterward was a realization that by avoiding the deeper levels of reflection, she was losing access to greater creativity in her life.

Another person reported that the last question was one he felt had just been waiting to come out all day. The space to hear the question was created in the exercise. He also reported that the exercise had changed his relationship to everyone in his small group. "All of a sudden, we became *we.*"

Tapping into the inner wisdom of the soul can be an emotional experience. We are moved by the magnificence of getting in touch with the essence of our being. In many cases, the people in these groups do not know each other very well. They are always amazed at how quickly they are able to go into a reflective mode and share from such a deep level in a nonthreatening way. They talk about the conversation as being authentic, genuine, deeply engaging. When our hearts connect, there are no strangers.

Oftentimes there are several groups participating in this exercise at the same time, all in the same room. Participants are surprised to discover that they can hear the people in their groups, even though the room gets noisy at times. They find that when they are truly listening, the external noise disappears. It is beautiful to watch, too. As one person is reflecting, the group leans back. Then as the person begins to speak, everyone in the group leans forward. It's like watching a living organism breathing.

If you are introducing this exercise to a group of people, it is your responsibility to make it safe. It can seem threatening for some people. You make it safe by explaining what is going to happen, by being vulnerable yourself, and by holding a sacred space. I can't tell you how to do this; it's more of an intention. When I visualize what I mean, I am standing there with my arms outstretched, embracing the whole room.

Once we experience this type of listening, we begin to see how powerful it can be. Physician Rachel Naomi Remen, in her book *Kitchen Table Wisdom,* writes about listening.

I suspect that the most basic and powerful way to connect to another person is to listen. Just listen. Perhaps the most important thing we ever give each other is our attention. And especially if it's given from the heart. When people are talking, there's no need to do anything but receive them. Just take them in. Listen to what they're saying. Care about it. Most times caring about it is even more important than understanding it. Most of us don't value ourselves or our love enough to know this. It has taken me a long time to believe in the power of saying, "I'm so sorry," when someone is in pain. And meaning it.

One of my patients told me that when she tried to tell her story people often interrupted to tell her that they once had something just like that happen to them. Subtly her pain became a story about themselves. Eventually she stopped talking to most people. It was just too lonely. We connect through listening.[3]

PRACTICE 2 • THE THREE BREATHS

After you have experienced the reflection process in the Listening Stick exercise, you might find this shorter version useful in your daily life—especially for times when things are getting out of control and you are ready to pop. It's called the Three Breaths. It can be used in the moment as a brief process to get centered and listen to the Self.

First breath: Inhale and identify what is upsetting you, controlling you, causing you stress.

Let go of it as you exhale.

Second breath: Inhale and touch the still point at the center of your being, the place you got to after your 20 to 30 seconds of reflection in the Listening Stick exercise. See whether you can get there with a breath.

Exhale.

Third breath: Inhale and ask yourself, "What is next?" It's tapping into your inner wisdom.

Exhale and notice what comes to your mind.

You will find that this very simple intervention will alter the path you were on when you felt stressed and out of control. You will approach the situation from a more centered place. The circumstances may remain exactly the same, but your response to them will be different.

One of the fruits of this exercise shows up as an appreciation for people being who they are. This occurs in personal relationships—for example, when a family member starts doing something that really irritates you. When you are conscious, you can step back a moment and look at that person and say to yourself: "That's just Bob being Bob. If he were being any other way right now, he wouldn't be Bob, he'd be who I'd like him to be or who I think he should be." And you begin to appreciate him for being who he is. At that point you can begin to listen to him in a new way. It's also a useful benefit in business meetings, when someone is going off in a direction that you really don't agree with or that you think is absurd. Once you remind yourself to appreciate in this way—it's just Mary being Mary—you can begin to hear the words she is saying from her perspective. It can make a big difference in relationships and in outcomes.

Reflective listening helps us practice discerning the wisdom of our inner voices. Some people talk about it as discerning the voice of God in our lives. It is a very powerful tool in accessing listening as an art. We can train ourselves in this practice by taking a few moments to reflect before responding to others in our everyday lives. As we get to know and respond to this voice, our lives begin to transform. We are able to come from a place of peace and knowing, regardless of the circumstances. We become more present to love, joy, and truth. We know we can tap into our inner resources at any time.

4

HEART LISTENING

Presence—listening from the heart, listening that connects us—is the third quality that supports the sacred art of listening. Deep listening occurs at the heart level. It is present when we feel most connected to another person or to a group of people. Our hearts expand and our capacity to communicate with those of differing beliefs and customs increases. This type of listening is also about hospitality: offering space where change can take place, where there's a freedom to be. It's being fully present with another person.

When hearts listen, angels sing.

—ANONYMOUS

Our culture is dominated by sight—think about the thousands of images we see each day on television, on the Internet, and in newspapers, magazines, and journals. Seeing and listening are very different. The substance of seeing is light, which moves at 186,000 miles per second. Sound, what we hear, travels at 1,100 feet per second. So to listen, we must slow down and operate at the speed of sound rather than at the speed of light. In addition, we speak at the rate of 125 to 250 words per minute. We can process speech at up to 500 words per minute, and we think at 1,000 to 3,000 words per minute. These facts explain why it's not so easy to stay tuned, to remain present to the speaker when there's so much going on in our minds.

Peter Senge, author of *The Fifth Discipline Fieldbook,* has this to say: "Generative listening is the art of developing deeper silences in yourself, so you can slow your mind's hearing to your ears' natural speed, and hear beneath the words to their meaning."[1]

Really listening is one of the best gifts one human can give another. It requires our full attention. It calls for a mind-set of appreciation, curiosity, and wonder for the other person. We can't be thinking about what we are going to say in response, or how we would handle the situation, or what's going on at work or at home. We must let go of our own agendas for the moment, which is not an easy thing to do.

Carl Rogers, the well-known psychologist, says: "To be with another in this way means that for the time being, you lay aside your own views and values in order to enter another's world without prejudice. In some sense it means that you lay aside yourself."[2] The Christian Bible refers to this kind of selflessness in the verse: "Put your life on the line for your friends" (John 15:15). Giving up our ego self to be present with others is like putting our lives on the line for them.

We are overwhelmed with distractions that interfere with listening.

Sound engineers have a vocabulary that distinguishes the signal from noise. The signal is the part of the transmission that is meaningful. Noise is all the unwanted stuff that interferes with the ability to hear and understand the signal. Sometimes it's hard for us to find the signal.

What do we do about all the things that keep us from being fully present, from hearing the signal? It's relatively easy to discern the external distractions: noise, the telephone, e-mail, dogs barking, children playing. Some distractions can be turned off; others can be noticed and set aside after we become aware of them. The internal distractions—the noise and chatter in our heads, the song or melody that we can't seem to shake, the worries, the tasks to do, our emotions—become so commonplace, we don't even notice them. Once we do, we can put the thoughts aside and listen for God's signal. Be still, quiet down, listen, be. Only when we come out of it do we realize that we have been in deep, profound silence, accessing the voice of our souls.

Practices

PRACTICE 1 • TAKE A MINDFULNESS MINUTE

What can we do to become more present? In a book called *The Zen of Listening,* author Rebecca Shafir recommends the practice of a mindfulness minute each day.[3]

Take 60 seconds to focus your attention on the present moment. Choose a mundane task that you do every day: taking a shower, brushing your teeth, preparing a meal, eating a meal. For example, as I'm brushing my teeth, my minute would go something like this: I pick up my toothpaste. I unscrew the cap. I put the cap on the counter. I turn on the water. I pick up my toothbrush. I wet it under the water. I squeeze the toothpaste onto my brush. I put the cap back on the toothpaste. I put the toothpaste back on the counter. I brush the teeth on the right side of my mouth, and so on. Continue this awareness for one full minute. Stay in the present tense the whole time.

The daily practice of taking a mindfulness minute helps us look at things that are mundane, ordinary, and everyday and see the richness in them. It trains our concentration, and our ability to listen in the present moment improves. For many people, the mindfulness minute becomes the one thing that they remember about what they did all day. We are so used to multitasking. We seem to think that the preferred mode is to do two or more things at the same time. New research by David E. Meyer at the University of Michigan is finding that chronic multitasking, in addition to being inefficient, can lead to a risk of brain damage. It's actually stressful on our bodies to bounce from task to task. We can't truly be in the present moment when we are focused on more than one thing at a time.

PRACTICE 2 • MINDFUL PHONE CALLS

Thich Nhat Hanh, the Vietnamese monk who teaches about mindfulness at his retreat center at Plum Village in France, has trained his staff to take two breaths before they answer the phone in his office. On the first breath they detach from the task they were doing. On the second breath they center themselves. Then they pick up the phone. By this time they are ready to give their full attention to the caller. All too often I find myself continuing to work on the computer, prepare a meal, put away the dishes, or read a report while I'm on the phone. In making these two breaths my daily practice, I find that my phone calls are much more satisfying—as well as more productive.

PRACTICE 3 • THE PRACTICE OF DIALOGUE

Another practice that trains us to listen with our hearts is the art of dialogue. The word *dialogue* is used a lot these days—but often it turns out to mean a serial monologue! You say what's on your mind, then I say what's on my mind, and we are not really listening to each other. It could just as easily be done by two tape recorders talking to each other. There is no interaction.

What do I mean by dialogue? The work that I do with dialogue comes from the writings of David Bohm, a quantum physicist, who is well known for his development of the implicate theory, a level of reality beyond our everyday thoughts and perceptions. He posited that the totality of existence is enfolded within each fragment of space and time, and thus everything in the universe affects everything else because all are part of the same unbroken whole. Thomas Merton says it another way: "There is in all visible things…a hidden wholeness."[4] Martin Luther King Jr. described it this way: "Whatever affects one directly, affects all indirectly."[5]

Dr. Bohm became interested in how humans learn and think, particularly collectively. What is the nature of human thought? What are the dynamics of group consciousness? He spent much of his later life in intense conversation with the spiritual teacher J. Krishnamurti, and over the years he developed a deep understanding about this process, which he called dialogue. One of the main features in understanding the process is knowing the distinction between dialogue and discussion.

Dialogue comes from the Greek *dia* (through) and *logos* (meaning or word). So a dialogue is a flow of meaning through words in which new understandings emerge that might not have been present before. It is done in a spirit of inquiry—wanting to know. We look for shared meaning beyond our individual understanding.

Discussion comes from the Latin *dis* (apart) and *quatare* (to shake). It has the same root word as *percussion* and *concussion*—to break things up. A discussion is an analysis, a search for an answer. It is done in the spirit of looking for results. Each person states his or her analysis of the situation with the hope of influencing the other's position on the issue.

One mode is not better than the other—both are valid means of communicating. It's simply helpful to know what kind of conversation you are engaging in. If one person is in the mode of a dialogue, wanting to explore an issue, and the other person is in the mode of discussion, looking for a solution to the issue, they are really in two different types of conversations. It's small wonder that each person feels unheard. The first person wants to know why the second is in such a rush to action; the second person is wondering why the first person can't make a decision. They are each listening for something different. They are not connecting. Once we identify this situation, we can decide whether we are ready to modify our way of being in the conversation or whether we need to describe the two types of communication for the other person and see whether he or she is willing to switch modes for a time. Listening to what kind of conversation we are in is not only useful, it is also a key to effective communication. The interplay between dialogue and discussion forms the dance of daily conversation. We simply need to know what dance we are in and learn the appropriate steps.

In addition, if we think about it, there are all sorts of topics that are not discussible. No one mentions them; they are just there underneath the surface, blocking deep heart-to-heart communication. A workshop participant shared his example about family gatherings that were most uncomfortable because one person always drank too much. Everyone in his family was aware of it, but no one would talk about it. Finally, one person broke through the silence. The participant said there was an almost audible sigh of relief that the family could finally talk about it. The person who was the subject of this conversation was able to hear his family, and he chose to get treatment.

The dialogue process provides a safe space for these conversations. If we are interested in bringing difficult issues to the surface to find a new flow of meaning, it's important to stay in this process. To do so, we need to understand the principles and practice the guidelines.

The safe space created by the dialogue process provides a container for these conversations. A dialogue slows down the conversation. We can take our time. We exercise the muscle of listening to others. The purpose of a dialogue is to:

- Come to a new understanding.
- Build community as a board, group, or team.
- Develop shared meanings.
- Hear each other's stories and recognize each other's gifts.
- Appreciate diversity and wisdom.
- Listen with a spiritual ear.
- Bring about healing.
- Understand our differences by talking about issues we find difficult. (Dialogue is a gentle way to get these topics on the table.)
- Create a culture that recognizes that we are all members of one family, the human family.
- Create communities of love. Love put into action and appealing to human goodness may be the key to healing our hearts.

What are the outcomes of dialogue? It creates a safe space, so it builds relationships and trust. We can unlearn misinformation about each other. We begin to discern our common values: what God wants us to do, what we are being called to do. We explore new areas of reality and beliefs that we hadn't thought about before. We tap into our collective wisdom.

Understanding leads to mutual respect:

The more we understand, the less we fear.
The less we fear, the more we risk.
The more we risk, the more we trust.
The more we trust, the more we love.

The Quakers practice a form of dialogue in their meetings. Two of their principles are:

Try to listen carefully that you might not have to speak.
It's a sin to speak if you're not moved to speak. It's a sin not to speak
   if you're moved to speak.

By listening carefully, we realize that if someone has already said what we were going to say, there is no need to repeat it. Noticing whether or not we are moved to speak is an excellent exercise in discernment.

We owe it to the community to speak if we are genuinely moved. If we fail to share what's most important to us, it can damage our relationships and lead to isolation and estrangement. If we are speaking just to hear ourselves talk, rather than because we are moved to speak, it also is a disservice to our community. It takes practice and patience to be able to discern this point.

The following principles are designed for use in groups. As we explore them, however, you will begin to notice that they relate to all areas of your life and that they are all an expression of love in action. They invite you to listen with a new ear, informed by what you've learned. When you use them, notice how the quality of your relationships changes.

These principles or guidelines remind us to stay in the present moment, to listen to others with our hearts. They are meant as a guide, not as a set of rules or commandments. Because we are all learning the practice of dialogue, we need to be gracious about reminding each other when we forget one of the guidelines.

Guideline 1: When you are listening, suspend assumptions. What we assume is often invisible to us. We assume that others have had the same experiences that we have had, and that's how we listen to them. Notice when you are surprised, upset, or annoyed by something someone else is saying. Those are clues that you may be making an assumption. Let it be—suspend it—and resume listening for an understanding of the other.

Assumptions are so transparent that it takes practice to recognize them. If I am surprised by something someone says, then I must have assumed that she was going to say something else. If I am upset by something, it is often because what was said is challenging to my beliefs or values, and it's easier to follow my emotion and my agenda than to let it go and simply listen to what the other person is saying, without assuming it's wrong or absurd. Often another viewpoint is simply different. Then I can recognize that my viewpoint may be based on assumptions that are not true.

Guideline 2: When you are speaking, express your personal response, informed by your tradition, beliefs, and practices. Speak for yourself. Use "I" language. Take ownership of what you say. Speak from your heart. Notice how often the phrases "we all," "of course," "everyone says," or "you know" come into your conversation. The only person you can truly speak for is yourself. Try to avoid "always" and "never."

This may be one of the most difficult principles to follow. In our culture we may be considered egocentric when we use the word "I." When I was growing up I was trained not to talk about myself, so it was a real challenge for me to be able to speak from my heart using "I" language. Once I realized that this "I" is not the ego but the heart, I found it much easier. Connection happens when we speak from our hearts. Notice the difference in these two examples:

> Everyone knows that when you are on a spiritual journey you have to explore other traditions. You have to find out what others believe to learn more about your own faith. Of course, you have to be open to new ideas in order to grow. We all know that's the way to expand our capacity to love.

> Part of my spiritual journey has been to explore many different traditions. In my experience the more I learn about what other faiths believe, the deeper I travel into my own faith

tradition. I find that as I'm open to new ideas, I grow and my capacity to love expands.

In the first example, someone is telling me about something that I have to do while remaining at a distance. In the second one, I'm hearing what's in someone's heart, not what's on her mind. This person is letting me know who she is, and I can relate.

Guideline 3: Listen and speak without judgment. The purpose of dialogue is to come to an understanding of the other, not to determine whether he or she is good, bad, right, or wrong. If you are sitting there thinking, "That's good," "That's bad," "I like that," "I don't like that," you are having a conversation in your own mind, and you are not listening to the speaker. Simply notice when you do this and return to listening to the speaker.

These conversations in our minds are nearly constant. With training, however, we can learn to let them go and return to listening to the speaker. Judging is not a bad thing. We need to be able to judge and evaluate on a daily basis. In this process, though, judging gets in the way of listening. As Mother Teresa said, "If you judge people, you have no time to love them."[6]

Guideline 4: Suspend status. Everyone is an equal partner in the inquiry. There is no seniority or hierarchy. All are colleagues with a mutual quest for insight and clarity. Each of us is an expert in our own lives, and that's what we bring to the dialogue process.

We cannot have a true dialogue if we give anyone in the circle special notice due to their position, education, economic status, age, or gender. It is the egalitarian nature of the dialogue that opens us up to new thinking. Each person must be able to speak freely, knowing that there will be no repercussions later. This does not mean that we all have to agree. We can learn to accept that we can be colleagues with different points of view.

Guideline 5: Honor confidentiality. Leave the names of the participants in the room so that if you share stories or ideas, the identities of participants will not be revealed. Create a safe space for self-expression. Avoid gossip.

This guideline is another aspect of ensuring the open nature of dialogue. Each person has to understand that what is shared in the circle will not be shared outside the circle. Someone once pointed out that we can share ideas by saying, "A wise person once said..." Another aspect of confidentiality is to allow what has been said in the circle to complete that conversation, rather than approach someone later to tell her your ideas about what she said. This also helps us avoid gossip about others. Simply hold each other in the Light, knowing that each one of us has our own inner teacher.

Guideline 6: Listen for understanding, not agreement or belief. You do not have to agree with or believe anything that is said. Your job is to listen for understanding, new ideas, and ways to think about something.

We are trained to listen for agreement or disagreement in our culture. If I agree with you, I listen for all the reasons that I support you. If I disagree, I listen for all the reasons that you are wrong. This guideline asks us simply to listen for understanding. The main purpose of being in a dialogue is to come to some new understanding. It's a challenge to listen in such a way that no matter what someone says, you do not have to believe it or agree with it to keep on listening and to be open to discovering new ways of thinking about something.

Guideline 7: Ask clarifying or open-ended questions to assist your understanding and to explore assumptions. Watch out for questions with your own agenda embedded in them.

Many times I notice that questions begin: "Don't you think that…?" Whatever follows is the agenda of the questioner, not really a clarifying or open-ended question. Notice this in interview shows. Many times the interviewer will start a question with "Don't you think…" and the interviewee will say: "No, that's not what I think. This is what I think." The point of a clarifying question is to find out more about what has been said, not to inject your own agenda. An authentic question often leads the speaker to understand better what his or her inner voice is trying to say. You may want to paraphrase to make sure you heard what someone said: "I want to make sure I understand what you are saying," or "Help me understand what you are saying."

Guideline 8: Honor silence and time for reflection. Notice what wants to be said rather than what you want to say. Allow time to take in what has been said.

Most conversations happen so quickly that there is no time for reflection. In the dialogue there may be many moments of silence, as we think and reflect on what has been said. As we are changed by what we hear, we may find that we have nothing to say or that what we thought we were going to say has altered. The whole idea of asking yourself a question before speaking is unusual. Silence and reflection also give time to notice the conversation as a whole, rather than just what we have said. This awareness keeps us moving the conversation along rather than repeating what has already been said.

Guideline 9: One person speaks at a time. Pay attention to the flow of the conversation. Notice what patterns emerge from the group. Watch that each person has an opportunity to speak, knowing that no one is required to speak.

One of the practices in this process is allowing each person to finish completely what he or she has to say before the next person speaks. It is not the time to offer advice or solutions for any problems raised. It is a time simply to hear what is being said, receiving the voice of another's soul, and to notice how the conversation is flowing.

At the close of the dialogue, each participant shares one idea or insight that he or she gained by participating in the dialogue. Ask the question: "What is one thought, idea, or insight that you will take away from this meeting?" This provides closure, which is often missing in meetings where there's no formal adjournment, where people just drift off with no sense that the circle has been closed, that the conversation is over. The question also grants each person the opportunity to say what value she or he gained from being at the meeting. We give the gift of our time to these gatherings, and asking this question acknowledges that there was value.

Heart listening is a very deep form of communication. It's natural to want to protect ourselves from getting too close until we know we can trust. The dialogue process is designed to build that trust so it becomes safe to share at a deep level. John S. Dunne, a theology professor at the University of Notre Dame, phrases it so well: "Our mind's desire is to know, to understand; but our heart's desire is intimacy, to be known, to be understood. To see God with our mind would be to know God, to understand God; but to see God with our heart would be to have a sense of being known by God, of being understood by God."[7]

5

Opening Space for Listening

Who are we as listeners? In addition to the practices in silence, reflection, and presence, we also need to look at how we are listening and what we are listening for. The way we listen to others has a clear impact on the quality and depth of the conversation.

Many times we think we already know what the other person is going to say, so we stop paying close attention. Or we listen to others with a voice going in our heads, which says, "I already know that," or "Yes, but what about this or what about that," or "That will never work," or "You have no idea," or "That's not right." You get the idea. It's as though we have a checklist for our listening, and everything we hear gets screened through the items on the list. There's not much space for the other person in this scenario. All the conversation is going on in our own heads. We aren't focused on what the other person is saying; we are paying attention to how the words fit into our checklist.

In addition, we have certain ways of listening to others based on some preconceived idea of what they are like. We have unconsciously prejudged them by the way they dress; the color or style of their hair;

their race, culture, age, or religion; where they live; what kind of work they do—and we listen to them through this filter of prejudgment as well. We box people into a certain way of being, based on these preconceptions, and that's the way we listen to them.

For example, have you ever noticed your instant reaction to someone whose clothes trigger a particular emotional response? It might be someone who dresses beautifully, who looks like a fashion model, or who is dressed in the latest teen fad. It can be a challenge to get beyond that image. There's no listening for them to be other than who we think they are based on their outfits. That doesn't leave much of an opening for their self-expression.

At other times someone will say or do something and we say to ourselves: "What a jerk!" or "She's so arrogant," or "What a stupid thing to say/do," or "What an airhead!" Our tendency is to take these comments and label people, so the next thing they say is heard through the filter of that label. There's not much chance for them to show up any other way. Most of these examples are based on negative comments, because they are the ones that get in the way of authentic communication.

Another way we filter what we hear is by assuming that the speaker wants us to respond in a certain way. We listen through a filter of wanting to fix the situation, so everything we hear is heard through "What can I do to fix it?" Other filters of this nature are giving advice, giving answers, looking for errors to correct, and offering our own opinion. Sometimes I will say something like this to the person who's listening to me: "I really just want you to listen. I'm not expecting you to give me any advice, fix the problem, or provide me with answers or your opinion. I need you to listen to me."

Margaret Wheatley tells a great story about this in her book, *Turning to One Another.*[1] She was at a gathering of women from many nations. Each one was invited to tell a story from her life. A black South African began to speak about the horror she experienced when she found her grandparents slaughtered in her village. In the presence of that deep pain, many of the women wanted to do something—to fix it, make it better, take away the pain. The speaker felt their compassion but also felt them closing in. She told them that she didn't need them to fix her. She just needed them to listen to her. There's something very healing about being listened to. The quality of our listening can have a profound impact.

Somehow we all sense when we are being listened to through these filters, and we shut down. We live up to the listener's expectations. We realize it's not safe to open up our hearts. There's a well-documented syndrome called the Pygmalion Effect, with which you might be familiar. Studies were done in two classrooms. One teacher was told that her students were not very intelligent, tended to do poorly, and were not very well behaved. The other teacher was told that his students were bright, hardworking, and successful. The teachers believed these assessments, although the division of the students into the two classrooms was entirely random. Soon the first group was doing poorly and the second group was excelling. The teachers responded to the students based on what they thought about them. The preconception that the teacher had was a more powerful predictor of the child's actual performance than IQ score, past performance, or home environment.

When we are truly listening to someone else, we detach from these filters. It's not as if they are going to go away—we simply let them drift into the background. The practices of silence, reflection, and presence are key to expanding our capacity to do so.

Once we get to know what we usually listen for, our own personal checklist of filters, it is easier to acknowledge the way we listen and then let it go so that we can be present with the person speaking.

Practices

PRACTICE 1 • IDENTIFYING FILTERS

Notice what your internal comments/assessments are, either out loud or to yourself, when you are listening to someone.

See whether you can identify your particular way of listening.

Experiment with opening up your listening.

Notice the characteristics that you hold out as benchmarks for judging what others are like.

Deliberately enter into a conversation with someone you would normally pass by: a homeless person, a youth with tattoos and body piercing, or someone from a different culture, race, or age group.

Notice what your filters are and when they disappear.

Our language and our listening create the space for what transpires.

Joseph Jaworski in his book *Synchronicity* says, "We do not describe the world we see, but we see the world we describe."[2] The way we listen to other people is the way they appear.

We also tend to listen for answers. "What do you mean?" "Where are we going?" "What are we going to do?" In deep listening we want to listen for responses. Each of us most likely has an answer right at our disposal when we are asked a question. The notion of waiting a moment to reflect never even occurs to us. The space for deep listening appears when we allow this to happen, both for ourselves and for others.

PRACTICE 2 • OPENING SPACE

When someone asks you a question, pause for three or four seconds before responding. If this feels awkward, you might say something like, "That's a good question. Let me take a moment to reflect before responding."

When you are listening to someone and he stops speaking, wait three or four seconds before you respond. The other person often has more to say, which will be lost if you jump in right away.

Sometimes we open up space for others to speak by saying what is true for ourselves. There's something freeing when the person you are with is authentic in the conversation. If I'm uncomfortable, I express that. If I have something on my mind that is interfering with my ability to be present, I speak the truth about it. The more I open my own heart, the more space there is for the other person to open her heart.

These practices will train you for deep listening. You will find yourselves more attentive to others in your life. You may be surprised at how they begin to appear to you. Once they realize you provide a safe space in which to open up, they will find a haven for their souls to reveal themselves. They will be empowered to express more of who they are. Quaker writer Douglas Steere expresses it this way: "To listen another's soul into a condition of disclosure and discovery may be almost the greatest service that any human being ever performs for another."[3]

The Physical Environment

One aspect of listening that is often neglected is the physical environment. What is it that supports deep conversation? How can we set up the space around us to nurture the sacred art of listening? I have found that paying attention to the physical environment and using rituals are two ways to respond to these questions.

First, we need to consider the physical environment, before people arrive. Whether there are only two people or one thousand, it is important to notice what the space looks like.

Is there a lot of clutter around? Papers, wastebaskets overflowing with trash, leftover cups from a previous meeting, dead or dying plants or flowers? Simplicity is the name of the game. Get rid of everything that isn't necessary. Make sure the room is neat.

Are pictures hanging crooked? Straighten them.

What is the lighting like? Do you need to open or close curtains or blinds? Do you need to turn on ceiling lights?

What is the temperature like? Locate the thermostat and adjust it accordingly.

What are the chairs like? If there are only two of you, sit in both chairs to get a sense of the space. Is it welcoming? A small, uncluttered round table is OK; desks are intimidating, so if you can, set up the chairs away from the desk, either facing each other or at a ninety-degree angle. The most effective position is one person sitting at 12 o'clock and the other at either 3 or 9 o'clock. The optimum distance between you should range from eighteen to thirty inches. Parallel eye level is best, so note the height of the chairs.

For a group, set chairs in a circle or in concentric circles. The maximum size of the first circle is usually 25 to 30 people. Leave enough space in between chairs so that people don't feel crowded. To get a sense of what participants will see, sit in chairs in the four quadrants of the circle. Look around and notice what you see. Does anything need to be moved? Are the chairs in the right part of the room?

Is there a lot of "white noise" from computers or copiers? Turn off what you can.

This may seem like a lot of busywork, but it really does make a difference. When people come into a room, their first impression sets a tone for how they respond the rest of the time. If someone has gone to the trouble of clearing the space, it somehow opens up an ambience that is comfortable and inviting. There is nothing in the physical environment to distract them.

Ritual is a way to create a special opening. When many of us hear the word *ritual* we think of something that is used in worship services. However, I expect most of us have a morning ritual, whether it's reading the paper, grabbing a cup of coffee, or brushing our teeth. These rituals are repeated patterns of meaningful acts that help us start our days. They can transform the ordinary into something special, acknowledging the presence of Spirit in daily life and in our work together.

Rituals provide us with ways to acknowledge the sacred or remind us of our purpose and that we have chosen to set aside time to participate in this particular conversation. Because each of us perceives things differently, rituals also help bring us together and we share a common experience.

Rituals often use symbols to represent an abstract idea. I use a candle and a flower, placed on a tray or low table in the center of the circle. The candle is the symbol for the first ritual. It represents light, Spirit, Creator, Source, life, fire. It is a common symbol in many religions. Lighting the candle is the ritual that acknowledges that the sacred is right here and now. It is a marker of our special time together. It is also a reminder for us to look for the light in each other throughout the session. "This symbol reminds us that even when the night is very dark, whether in our own life or in the life of humanity, [God's] love is a fire that never goes out."[4]

The second ritual has to do with the circle, which is why we arrange the chairs in a circle. Sitting in circles comes naturally to us. It is a very old tradition and has been part of our human community since the beginning of time. The circle is a universal symbol for unity and wholeness. Somehow I just don't see our ancestors sitting in rows, looking at the backs of heads! I think they were sitting in circles, most likely around a fire. There is a wonderful passage about circles from the Native American tradition, written by Black Elk.

> Everything the Power of the World does is done in a circle. The sky is round, and I have heard that the earth is round like a ball, and so are all the stars. The wind, in its greatest power, whirls. Birds make their nests in circles, for theirs is the same religion as ours. The sun comes forth and goes down again in a circle. The moon does the same, and both are round. Even the seasons form a great circle in their changing, and always come back again to where they were. The life of a man is a circle from childhood to childhood, and so it is in everything where power moves.[5]

The impact of the circle is very profound. It is also egalitarian. No one is at the head of the table.

The ritual consists of walking the circle. Walk around the outside of the circle as a way of calling it into being, drawing it, acknowledging it. Invite the participants to draw the circle with you by tracing the circle with their eyes and looking at the others who are there, as though seeing them for the first time. Acknowledge each other, send a silent welcome, appreciate each person as you look at her or him for taking the time to be there, and for being who she or he is. Look with a sense of wonder and curiosity. This ritual gives permission to really see each person in the room. It's very powerful to silently greet each other in this way.

The circle becomes the symbol of sacred space. We have declared it to be so.

The center of the circle is a symbol of common ground. We had to look across the center of the circle to see each person, so all eyes intersect in the center at some point, which is a way we find our common ground.

The flower on the tray next to the candle is a symbol of the beauty and order of nature. Often we sit indoors for our meetings, and this is a way to remember that there is a whole world of nature surrounding us, supporting us in our lives.

The ritual of calling the circle draws the boundary between social time and circle time. We connect. We see each other. Find a ritual that you can use at home or at work to remind yourself of the sacred in each moment.

One participant took this idea home with him and created a homecoming ritual by designating one part of a room as sacred space. His ritual was to spend the first five or ten minutes there after arriving home from work. He has two young children, and they quickly learned that this was Daddy's time. Some days they join him there, honoring the silence. He reported that this ritual created some of the best bonding with his children—in the silence together.

Another workshop participant had recently become engaged to be married. She decided to buy a special candle that she would light every time she sat down to plan for the wedding. She wanted to remind herself of the sacred nature of marriage and to keep Spirit in her mind as she dealt with all the details involved.

Opening up the space for listening to others can be as simple as opening up your heart. However, most of us need additional tools to help us create that safe space. These ideas provide a number of ways to sharpen our skills. As we practice noticing how we listen, what we are listening for, and the type of environment and rituals that are conducive to evoking heart-to-heart communication, we tap into the power of the sacred art of listening—to ourselves and to each other.

6

THE IMPACT OF LISTENING

You have probably heard (or used) the expression "What you need is a good talking to!" It's often said by someone who is frustrated in his or her ability to communicate or who thinks that more words will alter the other person's behavior. Oftentimes our problems arise because we aren't listening to the person who is frustrating us. Imagine how it would change the interaction if that person responded by saying, "What I really need is a good listening to." The recognition that listening has the power to transform our relationships just doesn't occur to us.

Whom would you like to impact with the quality of your listening? Think about a person, a group of people, or a situation that is puzzling you, concerning you, or important to you. It may be that you simply have a sense that there's something that needs to be said. Or that you have tried talking and nothing has changed. I ask this question at the beginning of my workshops as a way to expand ideas about listening. Many times participants mention family members or someone close to them. Some find it's a group that they are in or their professional relationships—teachers and students or therapists, lawyers, or doctors and clients.

I also ask myself whom I want to impact with my listening. There's always someone! It may be that something is missing in our communication, or I have a sense that the person wants to tell me something and doesn't know how to do so, or I realize that I have been giving advice or answers rather than empowering the person to discover the solution on his or her own. Once I have identified the person, he or she becomes part of the workshop. At some point, someone will share a story or I'll see something in a new way that relates to this person. As I listen more intentionally, the issue that needs to be brought out almost always comes up. Then, after the workshop, as I continue to just listen, the person usually comes up with the next action to take or the answer to the question she or he had. The quality of my listening opens up the space for the individual to find his or her own inner wisdom.

Most of us tend to think in terms of what we can say that will make a difference in a situation. We see speaking as the active role, doing something to shift a situation. I'm inviting you to consider the possibility that the quality of our listening can make an equally powerful difference. How we listen can actually alter someone's life.

Brenda Ueland, a journalist and author, tells a touching personal story. Her father was a person who talked a lot. He was a bright, witty raconteur who always had a lot to say. His relationship with her, however, was a lonely one, even though she knew he loved her. She didn't feel that he was at all interested in her, because he never stopped talking long enough to find out anything about her. She was just an audience for him. In his later years, Brenda found that her visits were marked by frustration, and she looked forward to the time she could leave. She kept hoping that he would ask her about her life and was disappointed when it never happened. He just couldn't listen.

Many years later, she received a letter from a family friend who had been aware of this situation, and he told Brenda that he was concerned that his relationship with his family had become just like hers with her father. They decided to get together for a weekend. By this time, Brenda had become very interested in the topic of listening and was writing articles about it. They went for walks and Brenda simply listened, without any expectation of being listened to. This went on for a couple of days, until finally he began to ask her some questions. She was able to point out the fact that it took him two days of talking before he asked her anything. She told him that if he was not able to listen, this might have something to do with his relationship with his children. His response was: "Now talk. Tell me about that. Tell me all about that."[1]

Two weeks later, she received a letter from him thanking her for the visit. He told her that he had discovered what original, courageous, independent children he had—and that he and his wife were enjoying a renewed relationship, talking about all kinds of things, making each other laugh again. Her listening had transformed his life. In Isaiah we hear: "Listen that you may live" (Isaiah 55:3).

There's something about being listened to, being able to tell our stories, that allows us to see the importance of our own lives. Sometimes we don't realize that we need to tell our stories until we talk about them with someone else. This is most obvious during times of high drama, such as when deaths, accidents, or health issues occur, or during special moments, including weddings and births. Then there are the everyday events that constitute a life. Each time we tell the story of what happened, we learn something new, or we get closer to healing a wound, or we remember another piece of it, or we gain a new insight, or we have a good laugh. A good listener encourages us and appreciates hearing our tales; we recall more and grow in our knowledge of who we are and what we are here to do. What a gift! Paul Tillich tells us: "The first duty of love is to listen."[2]

What is the impact of deep listening—both for others and for ourselves? There seems to be a built-in hunger to be listened to, to be nurtured by another's listening. We want to know that someone else understands who we are, our essence. The one we listen to often blossoms before our eyes, like stop-action photos of a flower blooming. The experience of being listened to assists us in a fuller expression of ourselves, allowing us to explore and understand who we are at a deeper level. In addition, telling our stories often gives strength and power to our convictions and leads us to act on something we are already engaged in or thinking about.

Once we understand how the power of listening can impact another's life, we will find many opportunities to practice it in our daily lives, as shown in the following examples.

This story happened more than fifty years ago. My friend had just returned to the United States after serving in the army. He was on a train heading back to Chicago, where he lived. He was standing in the corridor, looking out the window at the passing scene, the way he often did on trains in Europe. Several people passed by, but one woman stopped, curious that he was standing, rather than sitting. They started talking.

"How does it look to you out there?" she asked. He responded, "I've just come back from Europe, where things were so neat and clean. This looks messy and unkempt."

"Well," she said, "what are you going to do about it?"

This question startled him. He had already thought about a career in architecture or city planning, and this woman had listened to him in such a way that she knew the perfect question to ask. He has been working on the answer to that question ever since.

Another friend tells a similar story. A few years ago, she was at a personal growth workshop, where she was working on some issues she had identified in her life. During a break, she was having a rather casual conversation with one of the participants. He looked her right in the eye and said, "You need to go and find out about your roots." She was stunned. As a Native American brought up in a white culture, she didn't have much experience with her heritage. She knew this was the perfect quest for her. Since then, she has found a teacher, is learning the language of her tribe, and is very active in tribal affairs. All this growth stemmed from someone listening to her in such a way that he heard her heart's yearning.

Another person shared this story with me. "I remember a time when

I was worried and my mom said to me, 'I'm sorry I don't have a solution to the problem. All I can do is listen.' I was so grateful she didn't try to fix me or the problem. The next day I called her and said, 'Thank you so much just for listening. It was all I needed. You were really there for me and I love you for that.' I felt so connected to her in that moment. It is a moment I treasure, as I treasure my mom."

How do we become the kind of listener who has an impact? The qualities of silence, reflection, and listening are key to opening up the space for another person to be in deep conversation with us. Daily practice builds our capacity to be able to be in the silence, to know our own hearts, and to stay in the present. The previous examples all describe incidents in which someone was listening beneath the words to the heart of the other person. Even total strangers can listen to us in this way. The impact of being listened to is profound. In all three examples, the person who was listened to remembers the conversation word for word and was moved to action.

The very nature of listening implies that the listener will also be changed in some fashion. We will learn something new, or see another perspective, or find ourselves resonating with others, or realize that we could have another point of view on an issue. Focusing on someone else brings out the best in us. In some mysterious way, we contribute from the store of our life experiences, values, sorrows, wisdom, suffering. We share some of the same strength and insight as the person we are listening to. There's a sense of essence to essence. Connecting at this heart level touches us and leaves us in awe and reverence.

A friend told me this story, which happened at his weekly men's group. He had expressed some concern and anger about a particular issue. The group listened and then the next person spoke about something that was puzzling him. Then a third man talked about another issue. It was at this point, through listening to these two other men, that my friend realized he was not finished. He hadn't completed what was there for him to say. With this insight, he was able to continue to work through his anger and come to a more centered place.

I've had the experience of listening to people in other countries, where I don't even know the language. My husband is always amazed at how I can understand people when I can't understand their words. I am impacted by body language—and even some rudimentary sign language—and yet it's more than that. I anchor myself completely in the present moment. Somehow I connect with other people at a heart level—and our hearts speak the same language. It is a very active form of listening. Carl Rogers says: "When I have been listened to and when I have been heard, I am able to re-perceive my world in a new way and go on."[3]

Practices

Make a list of the people, a group, or a situation that you would like to impact with the quality of your listening.

Let go of any expectation about the outcome.

Be aware of the sacredness of each individual.

Choose one person or group or situation to focus on.

Prepare yourself to listen. Spend time in silence, get in touch with the still point of your inner wisdom, and open your heart.

Just listen.

Once you are alone, make a note of what happened.

What did you notice?

What was easy?

What was more challenging?

Once we learn how to make our minds still, like water in a pond, people are drawn to us. The stillness around us provides a mirror for them to see themselves in their essence, perhaps for the first time. This gift can transform a life.

7

LISTENING IN GROUPS

Community is one of the basic yearnings of humankind. We all seem to need that feeling of belonging somewhere. It begins in the family and then expands out into neighborhood, church or synagogue, school, work, volunteer activities, social groups, causes. We just naturally seem to gather together. Sometimes it's for comfort and solace, other times to take action. Sometimes it's for celebration and sharing joy, other times it's to connect, to be social, to be related.

Part of being in community is listening to others, applying the skills of listening one-on-one to a group. We often find ourselves in meetings: We meet to discuss our common concerns and issues; we meet to solve problems; we meet to create action plans; we meet to plan events; we meet to conduct business. We have a lot of meetings! How do we listen in a group? Everything we've learned about silence, reflection, and presence applies to listening in groups. We can also learn some new practices and ways of thinking about being in a group.

A circle is one of the key elements for facilitating listening in a group. Whenever possible, arrange chairs in a circle. It's really hard to hear others when you are seated in rows, and it's not possible to see everyone. Row seating also interferes with a sense of community and equality. Many people are not used to sitting in a circle, and it can feel uncomfortable at first. There's a sense of vulnerability—there's no place to hide.

Another aspect of sitting in a circle became clear to me a few years ago. I was attending a conference, and we had been sitting in a circle for all sessions for a couple of days. One evening we planned to have a celebration and talent show, so the chairs were arranged theater style. The moment we were sitting in rows, something happened. It seemed to invite a lot of side chatter, silly pranks, and childlike behavior. Sitting behind someone gave us permission to misbehave! It was as though we were waiting for a leader to call us to attention. It was fascinating. Sitting in a circle causes us to see ourselves and each other differently. There is no hiding, no mentality of being behind someone's back.

The flip side of this happened at another meeting. We began with a meal, so we were sitting at several rectangular tables. After we'd finished eating, the convener put a podium at the front of the room and opened the session. About halfway through we were ready to have a break, to be followed by a conversation about some future plans. I suggested that we switch to sitting in a circle. There was general agreement so we all started shuffling chairs and folding tables. When I looked around, there were two rows of chairs in about half the circle and several people were sitting behind the empty chairs. I asked someone to help me move the empty chairs. Those sitting in the "back row" were not particularly happy. They said that they liked to be in the back—more like observers than participants. The empty chairs provided that comfort for them. I acknowledged their concern and told them they didn't have to speak if they didn't want to. They could observe from their seats in the circle. Once they knew they had been heard, they accepted the removal of the second row.

Each one of us has a special gift or way of being to offer, and one of our jobs in life is to discern that gift and let it shine. Many tools have been developed to help us uncover our gifts. We all have one or more of some basic qualities, such as leadership or hospitality, or abilities in teaching, managing, caregiving, community-building, or problem-solving. What's germane to this conversation is knowing that all qualities are equally important, especially in groups. We need all members of the group there to make us whole. If one member is missing, the group is not complete. I have this vision of a sphere composed of an interconnecting web. Each member's gift is a strand of the web, and when one is missing the sphere is not whole. Those who are observers need to know that their gift is part of the whole, and it is not necessary to sit in the back to serve in that role. This is something to be aware of when we gather in groups. Each person's way of being adds to the whole. It may be more comfortable to be with people who all think just like we do, but then we are missing something, and no matter what we do, we aren't seeing the whole picture—and perhaps the one thing that would make the most difference.

Each one of us brings our own perspective to any group. Imagine that we are in a drawing class, sitting in a circle, and there is a still life in the middle of the room. Our assignment is to draw what we see. Each drawing would be different because we each see the same thing from a different angle. It doesn't mean that one of us is right and the rest are wrong. We simply have different perspectives.

All this points to the notion that when we are in groups, listening takes on a new dimension, which is appreciative of all our various styles. We begin to listen in a way that expands our learning together. The circle is an important element that encourages this growth.

The following guidelines support us in convening groups:

Arrange seating in a circle, without tables or desks, if possible. This creates an open space and promotes listening. Furniture can be a barrier to achieving open communication. Sometimes it's unavoidable. In that case, round tables are best; next would be a square configuration, with the least desirable a rectangle.

Start with 5 to 10 minutes of silence. This silent time provides a transition from the busy schedule of daily living to a more reflective state that is open to listening. It is a way to attune our hearts. As we sit in the silence, we slow down, begin to get in touch with our own inner wisdom, and start connecting with each other. We become present.

Go around the circle to check in with each other. What brought you here? What do you need to say to be present? The question will depend on the goal of the group or meeting. The purpose of doing this is to get in relationship, and it's the one thing that's missing from many meetings. We are concerned about getting through our agendas, taking care of business, and we think we don't have the time to check in with each other. In larger groups the check-in may be the only time that everyone gets to speak. There's something about making sure the energy of each voice is heard by the whole.

Many times we hardly know each other's names, much less anything about who people are. It makes a difference to me if I know that Ray got a traffic ticket on his way to the meeting, Susie's daughter is getting an award for her science experiment, Jane's mother is in the hospital, Larry just got a promotion, Kathy had to put down her dog yesterday, Don is waiting to hear the results of a biopsy, JoAnn is grateful for the beautiful day she had with her grandkids, and Ken is worried about getting laid off.

Yes, it does take time, as much as 45 minutes to an hour. We listen to each other with an appreciative and spiritual ear, we tell our stories, we share our highs and lows, we get to know each other. Then when we start our business agenda, we approach it from a different understanding of who we are as a group. The result is that the business usually gets handled in a much more efficient, effective manner. We are a collective body, rather than a collection of individuals.

Another variation on the check-in is to go around the circle and have each person say what she or he appreciates about the person on the left. It also promotes connection before moving on to business.

One of our jobs as members of a group is to listen to each other with respect. Remember that we don't have to agree with what the other person is saying in order to listen with respect. We also need to notice what's happening in the flow of the conversation, to be aware of the pace, to partner with the person leading the meeting. If you think the group is going off on a tangent, it's your responsibility to check it out with the whole group. It's OK to ask questions: "Can you remind me about the purpose of this meeting? Have we gone off track?"

If you notice that there are members who haven't spoken, let the group know that you would like to include everyone. "I'm feeling uncomfortable that only two or three voices are being heard. I'd like to hear what Michael and Sara have to say about this." "Can we go around the table to find out where we are at this point?" If you are discussing issues where a lot of people want to talk at once, designate someone to write names on a list as people raise their hands, so the chair can call upon them in order. If people are interrupting, cutting others off in midsentence, ask whether they can wait until the person finishes her thought. Sometimes it's important to take a time-out. "Can we have a moment of silence now?" As we listen, we learn that our contributions are not only what we think but also how we support the group to discover together the action or task it is being called to do.

I remember one meeting where a man was going on and on about one particular subject. The facilitator of the group was across the circle from him and was assessing the group's tolerance for this. The person sitting next to this man noticed and touched the man on the arm. He looked at her but kept on talking. She touched him again and made eye contact, at which point she told him that we were interested in what he was saying but there were others who also wanted to talk. He looked somewhat surprised and finished his thought and stopped. Afterward he told us that he had no idea he was going on so long. We need each other to remind us of our roles in meetings.

If we attend a meeting with the intention that we want to make a difference with our presence, we will look for the opportunity to do so. We can ask ourselves whether what we have to say is moving the conversation forward, or whether it is just a repeat of what's already been said. Ask yourself these questions: "What can I say that will contribute?" and "What can I say that will make a difference?"

Sometimes, when I am deeply listening during a meeting, I'll think of something I want to say. If someone else is already speaking I wait and listen. Many times that person will say what I was going to say—it's almost as though my listening and her speaking were connected. Then I don't have to repeat the thought, just continue listening.

Life has a way of keeping us on our toes by constantly changing. Sometimes we are called upon to discern that change. I find it useful to take some time to reflect on my membership in groups on a regular basis. The questions I ask myself are "Am I learning something?" and "Am I contributing something?" If the answer to both is no, then I know it's time for me to consider leaving that particular group. During my reflection, I look to see whether there is any reason for me to continue in that type of situation. Occasionally there is, usually due to a relationship that is important to me.

The practices of letting go to be silent, reflective, and present prepare us for listening in groups. They also prepare us to let go of a personal agenda or claim to a specific idea once it has been offered to the group. It becomes a product of the group at that point. It's not always easy to let go of "my" idea. I want credit for it! And yet, the good of the whole is for me to let it go. It reminds me of another Rilke quote:

> If I don't manage to fly, someone else will.
> The spirit wants only that there be flying.
> As to who happens to do it,
> She has only a passing interest.[1]

Listening is about relationships, how we get along with each other. It's really about opening up to love. There's a bumper sticker that says, "Listening—the language of love for everyone." It's sometimes easier to see that love during a one-on-one conversation. It's just as present in a group. The sense of holy, sacred moments when we are all part of the same whole is very powerful. Writer David Augsberger says it so well: "Being heard is so close to being loved that for the average person they are almost indistinguishable."[2]

In the past fifty to one hundred years, we have seen amazing advances in technology and mastery of the physical universe. Scientific research has taught us almost unbelievable things about our world. The problem is, it doesn't seem to have made much difference in how we treat each other. All we have to do is read the newspaper or watch the news. It seems to me that our job at this point in history is in the world of communication, listening, relationships, and love. Teilhard de Chardin wrote of this many years ago. "Someday, after mastering the winds, the waves, the tides and gravity, we shall harness for God the energies of love, and, for a second time in the history of the world, man will have discovered fire."[3]

Imagine a world in which we could resolve our differences without resorting to violence. How do we get there from here? Practice.

Practices

Notice the difference in atmosphere and energy when you are sitting in a circle, when you are sitting around a square or rectangular table, and when you are sitting in rows. How does each setting impact relationships in the group?

Request a minute of silence at the beginning of a meeting.

Take one minute after every meeting you attend to reflect on what happened. What lessons did you learn? What new insights opened up for you?

Make a list of each of the groups you belong to. Write down the purpose for each group. Prior to attending the next meeting for each group, ask yourself: What am I contributing to this group? What am I learning from this group? How can I support this group in reaching its goals? What is my commitment to this group?

Take a look at the agenda or topic for a meeting and be intentional about your participation to move the group forward. Sometimes a silent presence, holding the space for change, can make a huge difference. Other times you may find yourself speaking up, taking ownership of the group in a new way. Or you may find yourself supporting someone else in the group by your listening. The spiritual nature of these practices leads to a greater sense of community and connectedness. Creating community is a spiritual act.

8

LISTENING IN CONVERSATIONS

What is *conversation?* At the most basic level, it is a generic term for people talking together. A joke definition attributed to an anonymous source in an e-mail reads, "Conversation: A vocal competition in which the one who is catching his breath is called the listener." It may seem that way at times, and yet a good conversation—being able to connect with each other—is something we don't often experience. We yearn to be in community, and we haven't been taught the skills to discern how to listen and speak to each other.

If we carefully examine what happens when people talk to one another, we soon discover that there are many types of conversations— from formal to informal, casual to precise, simple to complex. Each one has rules, whether written or unwritten, and particular styles of speaking or jargon that determine boundaries for the conversation. The people most familiar with a particular kind of conversation know what the boundaries are and have implicitly agreed to keep within them. Those who don't know the rules often feel left out, not heard, or misunderstood.

Without the ability to distinguish these parameters, we often move back and forth between any number of conversations and wonder why we never seem to know exactly what's going on. As we examine these different types of conversations, we learn how to be more effective in our listening. We become aware of the many nuances of conversation and how to respond in ways that keep us connected.

A friend of mine tells the following story, which happened at a conference he attended. He found himself sitting at a table with a diverse group of people. A woman he didn't know was seated next to him and they began to talk. They found themselves with differing opinions and soon were in a heated conversation. By the time she left, he thought he'd violated just about every rule of civil discourse. He felt a little uncomfortable that he wouldn't be able to resolve his concern but didn't think he'd ever see this woman again, as she lived in another part of the country.

The conference ended the next morning, and people were milling about getting ready to leave. He noticed the woman across the room and wasn't sure how to respond because he was still worried that he had offended her. She waved in his direction—and he turned his head to see whom she was waving at. She repeated this gesture and he sensed that, indeed, she was greeting him. As she walked across the room toward him, he wondered whether she were going to harangue him about his rude behavior. When she reached him, she shook his hand, smiled, and thanked him for the wonderful conversation of the previous evening. She told him how much she had enjoyed the give-and-take and hoped that they would meet again. He was amazed! In her family this type of verbal sparring was prized. This was not the case in his family.

The woman was quite comfortable about the boundaries of the conversation. My friend didn't realize what they were, so he made an assumption about the impact of the conversation. This is a common occurrence for most of us. We assume that we know how our conversations are perceived, and we react without checking to see whether the other person has the same view.

Once my friend began to notice that the conversation was becoming an informal debate, he could have checked in with himself to see whether he felt comfortable with that. Then he could have checked with her, by saying something such as, "I'm noticing that the level of our conversation is getting more intense as we explore this topic. Is this OK with you?" Her response would most likely have been positive, thus sparing him the discomfort he endured and allowing him to really enjoy the verbal sparring.

Our families and backgrounds influence our styles of conversation, as evident in the preceding story. However, as we examine characteristics of conversation based on the topic and from the speaker's point of view, we discover that we already know many of the boundaries. We simply haven't been aware of them. The following inquiry offers one approach to a very complex issue as we explore three types of conversations: personal, information-based, and meetings.

Personal conversations are about the speaker's relationships. My purpose is to tell you or ask you something about me, something about you, or something about us. I want to share a story, solicit your advice, or give you information that pertains to my life, or I just want you to listen to me. Or I want to acknowledge you, support you, complain about something you've done that affects me, or ask you how you handled a situation that I am now faced with. Or I want to talk about something that involves both of us, which can be as simple as setting a time for us to go to the movies or as complicated as resolving a problem in our relationship. These conversations take place in our most intimate relationships and move across the whole line of family, friends, neighbors, community, and workplace. The tone can range from playful to serious. They occur daily.

Information-based conversations are more impersonal and have a specific result in mind. I need information on a specific topic, I want data for a certain project, or I have to place an order or make a request. Many of these conversations take place at work or in classrooms, although there are numerous opportunities for information gathering in any aspect of our lives as we go about our daily routines.

Meetings provide us with a third type of conversation. There is a broad spectrum of conduct in meetings, from the very formal Roberts Rules of Order to the casual leaderless groups that gather regularly around a particular agenda, such as prayer groups, crafters groups, and book groups. Language is formal and ritualized for many types of meetings. We really do need to know the rules in order to speak. Language can also be specific to the group. It seems as though each profession and interest group develops its own internal codes, abbreviations, and jargon.

There are even rules about networking—where to place your name badge, the amount of time you have to introduce yourself, what to do with business cards, when to move on, and how to work the room.

Once we identify what kind of conversation we are in, we have a much better idea of what the boundaries are; if we don't, we can observe and ask. We can also ask the other people what they would like from us in the conversation. Do they want us to listen, give advice, or provide information? The more we clarify what our roles are, the greater the opportunity for conversations that make a difference.

A friend of mine told me the following story: She was on the board of directors for a homeowner's association and had been feeling very frustrated about the tenor of the board meetings. One day it occurred to her that she was not in the same conversation as the rest of the board. She was in a dialogue, looking for new possibilities, and they were in a discussion, wanting to choose the answer from existing possibilities. Once she saw this, she was able to let go of her expectations for dialogue. Then she could participate in the conversation and make her contributions within the boundaries of a discussion.

All conversations can also be examined for the format in which they occur. The format can range from strict structure to very open-ended. It gives us the tools we use to converse. It informs us how to listen. The following list of some of the basic formats is designed to encourage you to examine the various structures of your conversations:

A *debate* is a formal contest of skill in reasoned argument, a discussion of opposing reasons. It is stylized and follows a specific structure. In a judged debate, each team is given a score for how well it stated its case. There is a winner and a loser.

An *argument* is a less formal version of a debate. Each side gives reasons offered for or against a proposition. There is no formal end to this conversation, so it's not always clear which side prevailed.

A *council* is a group conversation, when people gather to deliberate or form an opinion on issues that impact the whole. Government offers one form of this conversation, with city councils inviting public participation. It is a very formal structure.

A *consultation* is a less formal version of a council. People gather to discuss, plan, or decide something. Participants are invited for their expertise, and their task is to explore an issue and perhaps come up with some recommendations.

A *discussion* is a conversation in which each person presents and defends his or her viewpoint, pros and cons are considered, and a result is the outcome. It is important to reach a conclusion, to find an answer. When a discussion occurs in a meeting, there is a written agenda and each item on it is discussed and then voted on. In personal discussions, each person is often speaking to their own unwritten agenda.

A *dialogue* is an open-ended conversation of exploration and inquiry. It is a flowing of words and meanings to seek mutual understanding. A dialogue is open to new ideas and new ways of thinking. There are guidelines that help keep the conversation open. There is no expectation of a conclusive result beyond the expansion of understanding.

Brainstorming is a type of conversation in which the goal is to get as many ideas out in the open as possible. All thoughts are welcomed, with no judging or critiquing in the moment. The rapid pace of this conversation often leads to fresh approaches.

When we have sharp disagreements or differences of opinion, or when sides become entrenched, the conversation becomes a conflict. There is no giving from either side, and positions are polarized.

Negotiation is a conversation designed to reach an agreement between two parties that disagree. Each side is prepared to bargain to reach a result. A third party is sometimes brought in to facilitate an outcome.

Mediation is an intervention by a third party for settling differences with the consent of all involved. The parties agree to abide by an outcome put forward by the mediator.

Counsel is a mutual interchange of opinions and ideas, discussion, and deliberation. Often one person seeks the counsel of another to assist him or her in making a decision.

Social conversations are an informal way to communicate. We gather together and talk about whatever is on our minds. Depending on where we are, the rules of what's appropriate to talk about vary. Some social conversations never talk about anything that would be considered serious. Others have certain topics that they will tolerate and ones that are taboo. In some groups, for example, politics is an acceptable topic, but religion is not. In other groups it's just the opposite.

Chitchat is a very informal conversation that is light and superficial. It is not proper to ask a deep question. We talk about the weather or the traffic, tell jokes, and find out surface information about each other.

In any conversation the quality of our listening can help the speaker become clearer about what he or she is saying. We can also become more aware of the kind of conversation we are in and how we engage in it. Is this the conversation we want to be in? Is there some way to shift the conversation to be more productive?

Practices

PRACTICE 1 • CLARIFYING THE CONVERSATION

It takes practice to notice the various types and structures of any conversation. Prior to initiating a conversation ask yourself:

What is the purpose of this conversation? In other words, why are you seeking to talk about the topic?

Next, what is your intention for the conversation? What would you hope for as an outcome?

Finally, what are your assumptions going into the conversation? If you can identify them before you begin, you can then check them out to see whether they are accurate or the result of your own perspective.

A colleague shared the following story about a meeting that he chaired: He noticed that two participants were consistently the first to respond to any questions asked and were the ones making most of the recommendations. For various reasons, he didn't handle it at the time of the meeting. So he decided to call each person to check out his concerns. He chose to try this clarifying practice. Before making the calls, he wrote out the answers to the questions from this exercise for his own benefit. It was not a script for the conversation. This is what his answers looked like:

> The purpose of this conversation is to discuss what happened during our meeting last week.
>
> My intention for this conversation is that our meetings will be more productive as a result of new clarity about our expectations.
>
> My assumption is that you did not realize that others were not participating.

Once he was clear on what he wanted to learn from the calls, he said that it was much easier to let go of any uncomfortable feelings he had about making them. He wondered whether the partcipants would be upset that he was calling about this. Would they think it was not important? Then he made the calls. He told them the purpose of the call pretty much as he had written it down. After that, he described what he had noticed during the meeting and waited for their responses.

As it turned out, each particpant had been aware of the problem and stated that they had acted quickly to move things forward in a timely manner. Both of them agreed that they would be more conscious of allowing time for others to speak during their next meeting.

My colleague reported that the subsequent meeting had a completely different tone to it. The two participants waited and were not always the first to speak, thus giving the others an opportunity to initiate responses. He said it was almost as though the others were waiting for those two to speak and were somewhat surprised when there was silence. It took a while, but when the others in the meeting realized that it was their responsibility to speak up, they did. By being silent and waiting patiently, the two participants empowered everyone at the meeting.

PRACTICE 2 • IDENTIFYING CONVERSATION TYPES

Observe a couple of people or a group in conversation. Notice the type of conversation: Is it personal, information-based, or a meeting? Is it formal or informal? What structure or structures are being utilized?

Discerning the type of conversation we are in is another way to enhance our capacity to listen, make connections, and be in communion with one another. We practice by being silent, reflecting, and being present in the process. We are holy listeners.

9

DAILY PRACTICES

One of the keys to mastering the sacred art of listening is making a commitment to practice on a daily basis. It is tempting to think that by doing a little here and a little there we will hone our skills just as effectively as if we had a daily practice. There is no doubt that this method will have some impact on our capacity to listen. However, if we really want to be effective, we need to practice—every day. Remember the metaphor of artists, athletes, and musicians. All of them know the value of daily practice, endless rehearsals, and a regimen that supports their goals. They never stop practicing.

Another way to approach practicing is to understand that it's like exercising weak muscles. We start off doing a little and add more as we gain strength. Once we have developed that strength, it's there for us when we need it. At the moment we make a commitment to listen more effectively, we find that we are more attentive to others. However, often what happens is that when something comes up that presses our emotional buttons, we go to the default position of what we've always done in that situation. For example, imagine that you are in a conversation with a good friend or a business associate and he mentions something that you think is totally wrong. Your default might be to respond by telling him he is wrong or crazy or asking him how he could possibly come to that conclusion. With practice in letting go and being present, we can override the default so we can hear what is being said without going on the offensive or the defensive.

The following daily practices cover a variety of ways to develop your skill in the art of listening. You may find that some of them are already part of your daily life. Try out the ones that are new to you. Some may seem trivial at first, but the more you practice, the more you will find that each one opens up something within you that allows you to be a better listener—to God, to yourself, and to others. As you get to know yourself better, you will find you are more at peace and more receptive to being a listening presence in the world.

Choose one practice each day and focus on it throughout the day.

Notice which practices lead you to deeper conversations.

Incorporate them into your life.

Have fun!

Contemplative Listening

Find a minute or two at the beginning of your day to center yourself. Simply breathe in and out slowly and, as you do so, release your concerns to Spirit. Connect to the Spirit within.

Practice one minute of intentional silence to connect with Spirit. Look for a time in your daily routine that could easily be extended by a minute, such as before you get up, in your car, during a meal, or at bedtime. Tell yourself that this is your time to consciously listen in silence.

One of my colleagues told me about a man who claimed he had absolutely no time to be silent. Every second of his day was taken up with things to do. Finally she asked him whether he slept at night. He said yes. So she asked him whether he would be able to take that last minute before he fell asleep to practice intentional silence. He agreed to try. A couple of weeks later he called her and told her that he had taken her suggestion and found that it made him sleep better. Then he thought he'd try it at work, during the middle of the day. He discovered that he really looked forward to those minutes of intentional silence and that he was more effective at his work after taking a short break. It seemed to give him new ideas, relax his muscles, and renew his energy. He told her he was going to make the time to extend his silent periods. The value of silence had become clear to him.

Create a ritual to remind you to listen deeply. It might be lighting a candle or hanging a special poster or piece of artwork on the wall near your phone. Some people write notes to themselves and post them in strategic locations, such as by the telephone or computer. The note could simply have the word *listen* written on it.

Listen for the birds. Notice how many different sounds there are. You may not hear anything at first. It takes time for the brain to slow down enough to hear them.

Listen for small sounds: a cat purring, people breathing, leaves rustling. These are the sounds that train us to find the wisdom in silence.

Breathe in the scent of a flower, the air of the ocean, the richness of earth. This exercise connects us to nature.

Go for a walk and be mindful of each step. Notice everything that catches your eye and everything that you hear.

Start a spiritual practices journal. Write down the insights you gain from each practice.

Share a leaf or flower with a child. Children are filled with wonder and awe. They can see things that we adults take for granted.

Notice how often people say "you know." It may be a call for acknowledgment that they have been heard. It may really mean, "Do you know what I'm saying?" Become more attentive.

When you park your car, turn off the ignition and take one minute to be in the silence before getting out. This practice makes space for you to center yourself before going to work, running around on errands, or returning home.

When you notice your judging mind taking over, give yourself a time-out to pause and center. By getting in touch with your true self, you act from a place of connection and love for the world around you.

Savor the moments of centeredness. Acknowledge them with gratitude.

Find moments to pause, close your eyes, and become present to the silence within several times a day.

Find a way to create a mini-Sabbath—a time for renewing your soul. Pick an activity that nourishes you spiritually. Do it regularly.

Reflective Listening

Remind yourself that anything is possible. These simple exercises will help to get you outside the box of your thinking. I painted my toenails purple to remind me of this. I would look down at my feet and say to myself, "If my toenails are purple, then anything's possible."

Practice speaking from your true self. Own what you say by speaking for yourself, from your own experience. Use "I" language. Rephrase when you catch yourself in generalities.

Pay attention to the words you use. Notice how the way you use language impacts the way you feel. I am working on omitting violent and warlike words from my vocabulary, such as hate, kill, stupid, idiot, bombard, blast, and strangle. It takes a conscious effort.

Pay attention to what's true for you. Practice slowing down long enough to check in with your inner voice.

Be clear about what you want and let others know. Many times we are disappointed because things don't turn out the way we want them to, yet we have not let others know what we want.

For example, a couple of years ago I had a vision of what I wanted for Mother's Day, and I let my children know. They were delighted, and I had the nicest Mother's Day ever. (My son came to church with me, I had brunch with my daughter and two granddaughters, and I had dinner with another daughter after watching her perform in a play. My other son and daughter live out of town and we spoke on the phone.)

Practice asking yourself what wants to be said next. Reflect inward and tap the wisdom of your soul.

Say a prayer for those who irritate you. This practice can work miracles. These are the people whose phone calls you dread, or for whom you have to brace yourself for a meeting at which they will be present, or who have diametrically opposed viewpoints from yours.

When you find yourself closing down, imagine the person you are listening to as a four- or five-year-old child—sweet, innocent, and lovable. Hold that vision until you feel your heart opening up. You will find yourself listening to the person with compassion and becoming more able to connect at a heart level.

Become aware of times when you are not rushing from task to task and ask yourself questions. What is emerging now? What wants to be done now? You will begin to hear your inner wisdom as you tune in to the richness of life.

Reflect on your experiences. Ask yourself what lessons were there for you to learn. Write them in your journal.

When you are in a crowded public place, take a moment to look around you and appreciate the amazing diversity of the human form.

Heart Listening

When someone says "Thank you" to you, look the person in the eye and say, "You are welcome." Common responses to "Thank you" these days are "No problem," "It was nothing," and "Not at all." In a subtle way, these phrases deny the gratitude. By taking a moment to say "You are welcome," you connect with another person and acknowledge her expression of thanks.

When you aren't sure you heard something or if you don't know something the speaker assumes you do, ask for clarification. This is sometimes a hard practice, because we all want to seem knowledgeable or part of the in-group. I know I am embarrassed to ask when I think I should know something. I am training myself to ask. Much to my surprise, it usually creates a closer bond between the speaker and me. Our hearts meet.

When someone is speaking to you, stop what you are doing and listen. This seems like such a simple practice, and yet how many times do we continue what we were doing and listen with half our minds? It's actually more efficient to stop and listen than to try to do two things half-heartedly.

Create an intention for your day. For example, today my intention is to be at peace with whatever happens. Live into that intention.

Consciously express appreciation for others in your life. Use the words "I really appreciate the way you…"

When you are in a conversation and the other person stops speaking, wait three or four seconds before responding. You will find that he almost always has more to say. We are so used to the fast pace of conversation that we expect people to talk almost before we are finished speaking.

Notice the colors of nature—leaves, flowers, grass, trees. They are especially vivid after a rainstorm. Allow yourself to appreciate each shade and tone.

Notice the spiderwebs in the early morning when the sun is shining on them.

Find something to be grateful for each day. It can be as mundane as being thankful for running water, your favorite beverage for breakfast, the newspaper, the telephone, the Internet. Nature provides us with many opportunities to be grateful. Think about your family and friends, or your health.

Choose one task that you do each day and be fully present while you are doing it. For example, choose that each time the phone rings you will stop what you are doing, take a deep breath to center, and then answer it. Or decide you will smile at each person with whom you come in contact today.

Listen for connections. It's tempting to listen for how we are separate, different, and unique. Practice listening for commonalities, especially when the topic is volatile. It's all too easy to polarize the issues and demonize those who are on the other side. An example of this practice occurred with a group of Christians who had gathered to discuss issues around the topic of human sexuality. Many diverse opinions were represented. The group was divided into pairs who were asked to be in a conversation with each other until they found something they had in common. One of the pairs reported back that the only thing they found in common was that they had both been baptized. However, in the course of this discovery they did learn that they could talk to each other without demonizing and that they were beginning to respect each other.

Make eye contact and smile at the checker in the supermarket, the postal service worker, the clerks in stores, and the servers in restaurants. This is another exercise in connecting.

Take a different route home. Notice how you feel doing something new.

Say what's true for yourself. Speak your truth. This opens up space for others to share authentically.

When you are listening to someone and she finishes talking, ask the question, "Is there anything else?" Sometimes there is something right there, waiting to be said. Sometimes the person will reflect for a moment and then realize that there is more to say. It's OK to repeat the question after the next silence. Eventually, the answer will be "No."

Choose an intention for the week. Take the time to ask yourself who you would like to be for this week. For example, choose to be a person who laughs easily, a person who acknowledges other people, a person who keeps her word, a person who practices forgiveness. Really fix the intention in your mind. You might want to put one word on your daily calendar so you'll see it every time you look at your schedule. Then let it go. Don't focus on the word, simply know that this is your intention. It's a practice in being present.

Listen to a point of view that is different from yours without defending your position. It takes a lot of practice to be able to open enough space for this kind of listening. We are drawn to respond. If you must say something, try "I'll consider what you said." Or "That's an interesting way to think about it." Or "I can see how much this means to you." That's it. You aren't saying that you agree and you are acknowledging the communication. Just let it be. This is especially useful with emotional issues. It takes courage to listen to someone's pain and anger when it's about you, your family, or your culture, religion, or country. We each want to tell our side of the story, rather than listen with compassion. Most times the pain and anger continue, because people know the difference between when you are listening and when you are planning your defense.

Make a conscious effort to allow people to finish their sentences without interrupting them. When someone interrupts you, say, "I wasn't finished. Please hold your thought until I'm through."

Practice paraphrasing what you hear. Using your own words lets the speaker know that you have really understood his or her point.

Listen for the space between words. Remember that speech is slower than our thoughts, so it takes practice to slow the mind to the tempo of the words.

Listen to music without doing anything else. Allow yourself to be at one with the music.

Sing a song.

Memorize a poem.

Take a walk and notice everything you see.

Get involved in some kind of aerobic exercise. Sometimes we don't listen well because we actually cannot hear very well. Researchers have found that our hearing is protected and even improved through aerobic exercise! The researchers attribute this to improved circulation, blood-flow, and sensitivity to sound within the ear.

Ask others what you could do to improve your listening skills. This is risky, but honest feedback can be very useful in improving your skills.

Spend one minute each day imagining a world in which people spend as much time preparing to listen as they do preparing to speak.

Smile as you listen to your children. It's amazing how comforting this can be.

Ask, "How can I help you?" and wait for the response. You are calling forth the wisdom in another's soul by your attentive presence.

Spend one day acknowledging each person with whom you come in contact. Find something you can authentically say. Let go of any expectation of how this will be received or returned.

Use mundane, everyday tasks as opportunities to practice being present. Choose one task each day and notice your sensations: what you feel, see, and hear. Focus on one aspect of the chore at a time. Notice your breathing.

Remember the purpose of daily practicing: to prepare us to listen to God (contemplative listening), to self (reflective listening), and to others (heart listening). We become miracle workers for each other through the power of our listening.

10

Frequently Asked Questions

Listening as a sacred art not only takes practice, but it also raises questions. The following questions have been asked in my workshops and presentations. Most of them do not have a simple answer, nor do they fit neatly into categories. Responses come from my experience and my practice of taking time for silence, reflection, and presence. Listening is an ongoing conversation of learning. It takes patience and practice.

Contemplative Listening

What does "being centered" mean?

For me, it's about slowing down, being quiet, touching base with the central core of my being. Contemplative practices lead to this place. It is a quiet, grounded space, where I simply know that all is well. I am connected with Spirit. Once this practice is in place, I find that I begin to go through my day coming from that still place. There may be a lot of chaos around me, yet I am able to function with peace because I am centered in that space.

I didn't find the Taizé music at all peaceful. Is there something wrong with me?

Each of us has a unique path to the center. For some it's music; for others it's reading; for others it's something physical, such as walking or jogging. Musicians may have difficulty with music as a lead into silence. They tell me that they get caught up in the technical aspect of either the music itself or the performance, and it's hard for them to let go of that. Another friend found that she had difficulty using a prayer word. She is a writer and all words tend to lead her into her professional work. She began by using a simple image instead, for example, clouds or a lake or the ocean or the sky—a sacred gaze.

What can I do about my impatience with silence? And with granting others space to talk?

Both of these questions relate to practice. In a society that is as uncomfortable with silence as ours is, most people are very impatient with silence to begin with. Try being in silence in small doses. Practice the intentional minute of silence several times a day. Gradually increase the times of silence. As you become more at ease with silence, you will also find that it becomes easier to grant others the space to talk. The more intently I listen, the less I find that I have to say. I speak when I feel called to do so. As someone once said, "I have often regretted my speech, never my silence."

How do I access deep listening—to myself and to others?

The practice of contemplative listening will teach you how to let go of your thoughts so you can be a blank tape for others to speak to. When you are listening deeply to another, you will not be listening to yourself. At that moment you are the receptacle for someone else's speaking. When it is your turn to talk, the practices for reflective listening come into play, as you take time to ask questions and reflect before you speak. Be patient. Remember you are learning to tune in to your inner wisdom. It will become easier over time.

When I do Centering Prayer, the thoughts just keep coming—I can't stop them.

I'm not sure we can stop thoughts. I sometimes wish we'd been born with a mute button for our thoughts. Because we weren't, the guidelines for Centering Prayer suggest that whenever we notice these thoughts, we should gently introduce our prayer word, which symbolizes our intention to be in the present with God. If there are a lot of thoughts, we get to express our intention a lot. I was also told not to worry if some days are like that. It is simply God cleaning house in our minds! The more we practice letting go of our thoughts, the less disturbed we become when we notice them. Over time, it's easier to let them recede into the background and disappear from our consciousness. All we have to remember is to let them go.

I like doing Centering Prayer alone, rather than in a group.

Most of us practice alone on a daily basis. Each person has her or his own unique experience with Centering Prayer. Some prefer being by themselves. Others find that the energy of being in a group adds a special dimension to their prayer period. The main thing is to do it.

What happens when I slow down? Will I ever get everything done?

It's amazing what happens when we slow down to prepare ourselves to listen. Time takes on a different quality. Yes, the minutes on the clock still tick by, but we are not constrained by them. There's a freedom in slowing down. And here's the surprise—once we get back into our tasks and daily chores, we do them more efficiently and effectively. There's a cycle in which slowing down leads to action, which leads to slowing down, which leads to action, and so on.

A clergy friend of mine says that on routine days he meditates once. When his schedule gets a little busier, he meditates twice, and when it gets out of control, he meditates at least three times. He knows that the more he has to do, the more he benefits from the slowing down of silence, tapping into the wisdom, and coming from a centered place.

Reflective Listening

What is the source of the questions from within?

When we are reflecting and seeking the source of our wisdom, our inner voices, I believe that we are connecting with the Holy Spirit, Divine Wisdom. We have to listen to hear that voice, we have to pause and reflect to hear that voice. It is that which connects all of us. In the fast pace of our lives it's easy to miss the guidance that is there for us always.

"Notice what wants to be said"—how do I do that?

Again, it comes with practice—the practices of slowing down, reflecting, and being present. In listening for what wants to be said, I have to be fully aware of the present moment, and what's already been said. Then I need to get very quiet and silently ask the question. At that point my job is simply to be in that silence, letting go of my own concerns and considerations, allowing what wants to be said next to emerge.

What is the relationship between intuition and inner reflection?

Inner reflection prepares us for paying attention to our intuition. Intuition is a secular way to describe inner wisdom—getting to know your inner voice, the voice of your soul speaking to you.

Sometimes it's hard to get a word in edgewise. How can I get to talk?

It's become quite common in our culture for people to cut each other off in midsentence. Most of the time we are not even aware that's what we are doing. If you are not comfortable interrupting others, there's no opening for you to talk. One practice is to call for a time-out and express your concern: "I have something I'd like to add to this conversation and I'm finding it difficult to enter in. Could we slow down a bit?"

How can I be a better listener to my partner? How can I let him know that I am listening to him, without having to put in my opinion?

First of all, pay attention. Stop whatever you are doing to be with him. Let go of all of your considerations and simply be present. Look at him, nod, and use appropriate body language to let him know you are paying attention. Get in a mind-set of appreciative fascination. See whether you can view him as if you don't really know what he's thinking and you're curious to find out. Give up your agenda for the moment. Forget about offering advice or help. Just listen. It takes practice and patience to develop these qualities. (The person who asked this question happened to be a woman. My response is the same when men ask this question about their partners.)

How can I listen to someone and not imply that I agree with her?

First of all, really listen to her. Let go of all of your reasons for disagreeing with her while she is speaking. Let her know that she has been heard. One message you can give that doesn't imply agreement is, "I'll consider what you said." Other times you might want to say: "That is interesting. I can see how much it means to you." You do not have to say that you totally disagree with her. If she asks you what you think, state your position as calmly as you can. It's our emotional attachments to our positions that get us in trouble.

My coworker is constantly interrupting me with her incessant talking. How do I let her know that I'd like to listen to her, just not all the time?

We have become very lax in using good manners when it comes to conversations. It's almost acceptable to pop your head in the door and start talking, rather than asking whether it's a good time to talk. We do this on the telephone, too, assuming that if the person answered the phone she has time to talk. Model the behavior you'd like to see. Learn to ask: "Is this a good time for you to talk?" or "Do you have a few minutes? I have a concern (or question, or comment) about…" Give the person an idea of what you'd like to discuss, so he or she can make an informed choice about the time available. When your coworker interrupts you, tell her that you'd like to hear what she is saying, but you are in the middle of a project (or whatever is the truth), and schedule a time when you can talk.

My husband and I share tandem offices—he has to walk through mine to reach his. It's easy for each of us to forget that the other might be engrossed in a project and blithely ask a question or make a comment and expect an immediate response. We have learned to remind each other to ask whether it's a good time to talk before we jump in.

Heart Listening

How do you end a deep conversation?

One of the missing pieces in our culture is the ability to create closure. Many times we move from a deep conversation into routine daily chores so quickly that it's as though that meaningful time never happened. I like to take a moment with the other person, to check in to see whether each of us has completed what we had to say. (I say, "Is there anything else?" and then wait.) Then spend a few moments in silence. Take the next minute or so to thank and acknowledge each other. ("Thank you for listening to me," "I really appreciate the way you...." or "You really touched my heart." Say whatever is there for you.) Depart with a handshake, hug, kiss, or whatever is appropriate.

How can we listen for collective wisdom?

Listening for collective wisdom requires a deep silence within and an intention to seek the wisdom of the group. The discipline of practicing silence, reflection, and presence supports this intention. It's asking the question "What wants to happen next?" and listening in the silence that follows. It means paying attention to what each person says and not getting caught up by your own thoughts or emotions. It means listening outside yourself.

Is it OK to take a time-out in a conversation?

Many times a conversation will become so rich and intense that it's hard to stay present. Often people will ask for a time-out for silence or prayer. Occasionally a longer break is needed—maybe half an hour or more. Just make sure you have an understanding that the conversation is not over, and that you wish to complete it with details of when and where you will resume.

How much does body language matter?

Reading body language is one of the many tools that help us listen more effectively. The impact of someone else's body language can be very subtle. When I am speaking, I am not always aware of the other person's body language, unless it's obviously exhibiting an emotion or disinterest. When I am listening, the way I sit or stand sends a message of how much attention I am giving and how open I am. I usually try to sit in a relaxed position, with my hands loose, not folded together, and my legs not crossed; I lean forward and use appropriate eye contact. This makes me more intentional in my listening. Noticing the speaker's body language can be useful in keeping me present in the conversation.

What about cultural differences?

There are cultural differences in the way we speak and listen. In some cultures eye contact is considered rude. In other cultures everyone talking at once is the norm. Even the comfort zone of how close we are to each other varies from culture to culture. That said, it is my experience that when two people engage in listening deeply to each other, it's pretty much the same experience in all cultures. The art of listening occurs in that timeless space of presence, when two hearts connect. That is a universal experience.

How do I stop cross talk?

Cross talk, or talking back and forth and sometimes over and around each other, is a normal part of everyday conversation. There are no written rules—it simply happens that way. When we are desirous of a deeper type of conversation, we need to ask for what we want by setting up some guidelines. Using a talking piece is one way to practice having a conversation without cross talk. The only person who can speak is the one holding the talking piece. The talking piece can be any item that can easily be held and passed around. I often use a polished stone. Other suitable items are a feather, a bell, a flower, or a stick.

What can I do about people who talk too much?

Sometimes people talk a lot because they feel that no one is listening to them, and it becomes a vicious circle. In these cases, making the effort to listen as long as it takes, with no expectation of being listened to in return, will generally allow the person to slow down and listen.

A woman in one of my workshops shared this experience. Her father had always been a talker, and it bothered her a lot. He had a bout with a serious illness so she started thinking about life without him. She had an epiphany, as she realized that what she would miss most would be his constant talking. It made him who he is. Now she appreciates him for being a talker, and she is no longer annoyed by it. By accepting him, she is able to listen with more love and compassion.

Sometimes we do need to set boundaries and agree to listen for a specific amount of time: "Jane, I have fifteen minutes to give you my full attention, then I must get back to my work." Or say, "I wish I had more time to talk, but I just can't do it right now. Can we meet for coffee this weekend (or after work, or for lunch) instead?" But offer this only if you really mean it and are ready to follow through.

Another woman related a situation with a friend who did most of the talking in their conversations. She gradually realized that her part of the relationship was to be the listener and to let go of any expectation that she would be listened to. Once she saw this, she was able to own her role as listener and accept it.

How do I "begin to notice the flow of the conversation"? What does that mean?

Noticing the flow of a conversation means listening to yourself and others and paying attention to the content and the pace. It means noticing when someone is monopolizing the time and when others are silent. It means looking for patterns and themes and new questions. This takes practice. Begin by being aware—letting go of the conversations that start in your head—and always returning to the present moment. Ask yourself the question: What's happening now?

How do I listen to someone who is telling me things that are difficult to hear?

This is where practice in letting go can really make a difference. It's not easy to hear things that we'd rather not know, or reasons behind another's position opposite from ours, or things that are just plain disturbing. Having the space to listen without reacting negatively is a gift we can choose to give. Knowing that we don't have to respond is a big help. It gives us the freedom to simply listen. Giving up the urge to want to fix someone or some situation is another freedom. What we are striving for here is to be a listening presence. See the other person as a fellow human being who needs to tell you something. Send love and compassion to him or her. Pray for wisdom to listen patiently.

How do I let people know I'm listening to them?

First of all, you stop whatever you are doing to be fully present with them. Keep yourself from doing anything else, whether it's folding papers, preparing a meal, filing papers, needlework, or fiddling with something. It really distracts the speaker and gives the idea that you aren't truly there. Be aware of your body language, as discussed in a previous question. Finally, let people know what you heard them say, not what you feel about what they said. This is not the time to give advice, opinions, answers, or corrections. It is simply letting them know that their message has been received. Period. It's all too easy to jump in with our ideas about what they've said. This is a practice in slowing down, with total attention on the other person, accepting him without judgment, trusting that he has the capacity to handle whatever he is working on. It is being in the mind-set of wanting to know and understand.

How can I make people listen to me?

One answer to this question is that you can't make anyone listen to you. You can change the way you listen, but you cannot change the way anyone else listens. What I have found, though, is that the way you listen to others often has an impact on how they listen to you in return. In a way, you model the behavior you'd like to see in them. It's another way of expressing the Golden Rule.

Another answer to this question is that you must take responsibility to find out whether the other person is available to listen to you. Ask the person: "Do you have a few minutes to talk? I have something I'd really like to say to you. When would be a good time?"

You will also find more receptive listeners if you have practiced the qualities of silence, reflection, and presence. Your speaking will come from a more centered place and your authenticity will attract deeper listening.

Appendix I

Guidelines for Practicing Centering Prayer

Centering Prayer invites all on a spiritual path to sit in the silence, guided by your own principles of faith and understanding, with an intention to be present to Presence.

Posture

For most, the best posture is sitting comfortably with both feet on the floor, hands resting on the lap, and eyes gently closed. The aim is to let the body rest deeply during the centering, wholly relaxed and supported.

Centering

1. Take a moment to quiet down. Let faith and love of God's Presence be at the center of your being.

2. To dwell in this state of Presence, choose a word (a love word, a prayer word, or a sacred word—for example, love, hope, grace, *abba,* peace) as a symbol that expresses your intention to be with God. Gently introduce your word, supporting your consent to be in this Presence.

3. Whenever you become aware of anything else (thoughts, feelings, sounds, sensations, etc.), simply, gently return to the Presence with the use of your word.

Ending

When you have finished, let peace flow up to the conscious levels of your being by returning slowly to the present moment, gradually opening your eyes. Sit for another minute or two before moving on to your daily routine. If you are in a group, the leader may recite a prayer or a phrase or may sound a chime to indicate the time is over.

Appendix II

Listening Stick Exercise

This exercise is designed to:

- Give you a profound experience of deep listening—to your inner self (your soul) and to the soul of others.
- Create an awareness of listening and being listened to.
- Deepen your respect for others.
- Develop a sense of community.

Opening

Divide into small groups of four or five.

Invite someone to be first in each small group. Give this person the listening stick. (A marker, pencil, or any small round object, such as a stone, may be used.)

Explain the exercise and then demonstrate it. (See Listening Stick Exercise: Modeling a Response to a Question for a modeled response.)

1. If you are the person holding the listening stick, state the question to which you will respond. (The first question is generated in the demonstration.)

2. Close your eyes and reflect on the question (at least 20 to 30 seconds). Look for your response rather than for the answer.

3. Notice your immediate response. Go deeper. Trust your intuition.

4. Open your eyes and speak to your group. Say whatever comes to your mind in response to the question. Take as much time as you need to say what there is to be said.

5. When you're finished, reflect again. Close your eyes and go back inside and ask yourself: "What's the next question that wants to be asked?" It will come to you. This is not a linear exercise, so the question may or may not relate to what you've just said. Listen for the question without thinking about who will be responding to it.

6. Open your eyes and state the question that comes to you and pass the listening stick to the person on your left, who will respond to the new question and repeat the process. The last person to respond also generates a question, even though the exercise stops at that point.

Note: When you're not holding the listening stick, your job is to listen to what is being said. It is not a time for you to respond to what has been said or to ask questions. Listen for each other's souls. You may find yourself doing your own reflection during the times of silence. Notice that your response may be very different. Notice how your mind may wander when someone else is speaking. Train yourself to be present. Practice undivided attention.

Closing

When everyone has finished, acknowledge and thank one another. Gather in the larger group and reflect on the experience. What was it like for you? What did you hear? What did you notice about the process? What opened up for you?

LISTENING STICK EXERCISE: MODELING A RESPONSE TO A QUESTION

This is a verbatim response from a recent workshop.
Question: "What was the happiest day in your life?"
My response: "What was the happiest day in my life?"
Reflection period of 20 to 30 seconds.
My response: "My first response was to go through a laundry list of all the days in my life that were happy days. There were so many, so I thought—that's not it—and reflected further. I kept going by being with the question. What I noticed is that I kept getting to the present moment. It just kept coming up to the present moment all the time. I can't pick one of the days, and this moment recognizes that this moment has the possibility to be the happiest moment of my life. This is the moment now. What I have is now. To notice that this is the moment now is the moment that can be the happiest moment of my life. It's a reminder to do that. In reflecting on this question I became much more aware of being present in the moment—recognizing it, acknowledging it, choosing it. I have a choice each moment. [Then there was a pause while I checked in with myself.] I think that's all I have to say for now."

Reflection period of 20 to 30 seconds, where I asked myself: "What's the next question that wants to be asked?"

My response: "The next question that wants to be asked is, What gives you peace?"

Appendix III

Principles of Dialogue

Opening

Arrange seating in a circle, without tables or desks. This creates an open space and promotes listening. Start with 5 to 10 minutes of silence. This provides a transition from the busy schedule of daily living to an opening for reflection and listening. Go around the circle to check in with each other. What brought you here? What do you need to say to be present?

Principles

Begin each session by reading and/or talking about the principles. This is one way to incorporate newcomers and to remind people of their agreement to use these principles.

1. When you are listening, suspend assumptions. What we assume is often invisible to us. We assume that others have had the same experiences that we have and that's how we listen to them. Learn to recognize assumptions by noticing when you are surprised, upset, or annoyed by

something someone else is saying. These are clues that you may be making an assumption. Let it be—suspend it—and resume listening for understanding of the other.

2. When you are speaking, express your personal response, informed by your tradition, beliefs, and practices. Speak for yourself. Use "I" language. Take ownership of what you say. Speak from your heart. Notice how often the phrases "we all," "of course," "everyone says," or "you know" come into your conversation. The only person you can truly speak for is yourself.

3. Listen and speak without judgment. The purpose of dialogue is to come to an understanding of the other, not to determine whether she is good, bad, right, or wrong. If you are sitting there thinking, "That's good," "That's bad," "I like that," "I don't like that," you are having a conversation in your own mind, and you are not listening to the speaker. Simply notice when you do this and return to listening to the speaker.

4. Suspend status. Everyone is an equal partner in the inquiry. There is no seniority or hierarchy. All are colleagues with a mutual quest for insight and clarity. Each of us is an expert in our own lives, and that's what we bring to the dialogue process.

5. Honor confidentiality. Leave the names of the participants in the room, so that if you share stories or ideas, the identities of participants will not be revealed. Create a safe space for self-expression. Avoid gossip.

6. Listen for understanding, not agreement or belief. You do not have to agree with or believe anything that is said. Your job is to listen for understanding, new ideas, and ways to think about something.

7. Ask clarifying or open-ended questions to assist your understanding and to explore assumptions. Watch out for questions with your own agenda embedded in them.

8. Honor silence and time for reflection. Notice what wants to be said rather than what you want to say. Allow time to take in what has been said.

9. One person speaks at a time. Pay attention to the flow of the conversation. Notice what patterns emerge from the group. Watch that each person has an opportunity to speak, knowing that no one is required to speak.

Closing

At the close of the dialogue, each participant shares one idea, insight, or learning that he or she gained by participating in the dialogue.

Appendix IV

Interfaith Café

The Interfaith Café is a format for interfaith gatherings that I designed for the Alliance for Spiritual Community and the Religious Diversity Faire. It grew out of a hunger for small group dialogue. My twelve years of experience in interfaith work and events has taught me that the most meaningful experiences occur in small groups. The energy and excitement generated is almost palpable. "Let's do this more often!" is a common response. What we've discovered is that we need some help to get this kind of conversation going. The Interfaith Café was designed to provide a minimum amount of structure and a safe space. It draws on the work of Juanita Brown and David Isaacs and The World Café.

Set up the room in small circles of four to six chairs. Place some note pads or three-by-five-inch index cards and pens in the center of each circle. To ensure that people sit with others they don't know, number or label each small group. As participants arrive, have them pick a number or name to determine where they will sit. Most people find this a comfortable way to form diverse groups.

You might find it helpful to create one or two questions for the groups to use as they begin the conversation. A list of some that we have used is at the end of this section.

It is useful to designate a host for each group ahead of time. If possible, have a brief training session with them prior to the start of the café and go over the principles of the café and the guidelines for hosts.

What follows is a guide to creating an Interfaith Café, with an introduction to the café, explanation of café etiquette, format for the day, sample timeline, information on café etiquette, and guidelines for group hosts.

Introduction to Interfaith Café

Welcome to the Interfaith Café. (Introduce yourself and the hosts. Thank them.) I also want to acknowledge you for being here, for taking the time out of your busy day to spend some time in conversation. We all have many choices of how we spend our time. We are delighted that you chose to be with us today. If you brought literature to share, please use the display table. We ask that you not pass it around in your small groups.

One of the things we have learned over the past few years is the value of small group conversations. When we sit together and talk about what's important to us, our world begins to change, we become more alive, we tap into hope. Sewing circles and committees of correspondence helped birth America; conversations in cafés and salons spawned the French Revolution. Study circles created the massive changes in economic and social policies in northern Europe.

This café setting invites that kind of conversation and collective reflection.

Even though we lead busy lives, with more to do than we can ever get done, something's missing. We still yearn for community. We are hungry to tell our stories. In days gone by, this happened on front porches, in pubs, or in coffeehouses. There were unwritten rules for these conversations. No one wrote them down, and yet everyone knew the boundaries.

Today we live in one of the most diverse nations in the world. We come from all over the world and we practice a multitude of faith traditions. So to make sure that we all know the boundaries of how to be in this conversation, we have created Café Etiquette.

Explanation of Café Etiquette

We chose the word *etiquette* for a reason—it is about good manners, being polite, and creating a space for everyone to be heard. So we invite you to take this on in your groups and try them out for the time we are together.

There are only three guidelines:

1. Speak from your heart. Use "I" statements. This conversation is a sharing from our hearts, not a debate, so we invite you to own what you say with your language. Speak from your own experience, not from or for anyone else. Watch for "everyone knows," "we all know," "of course," or use of the word "you."

2. Listen with respect. Listen for understanding, not necessarily for agreement or belief. You don't have to agree with or believe what someone is saying to listen with respect. This also means no cross talk and one person speaks at a time.

3. Discover and explore. Listen for patterns, themes, new questions.

Notice what's being said instead of rehearsing what you are going to say. Keep an open mind. Be curious about others. Appreciate the differences.

Format for the Day

Each group has a café host, who has a copy of the etiquette and the questions for the dialogue.

You will begin with brief introductions, so you'll know who everyone in your circle is, where he or she is from, and his or her faith tradition or spiritual path. Then you'll review the etiquette guidelines and be asked to abide by them during your conversation. Your host will state the questions and invite the dialogue to begin.

You will have 45 minutes for everyone to speak. You'll get a 5-minute warning prior to the end of the time for the first dialogue. The next 5 minutes will be an opportunity to notice what happened during the dialogue. What themes or patterns emerged? What new questions came up? Use the notepads or cards to write them down.

At this point the café facilitator will invite one or two of each group to stand up to become ambassadors to two other groups. Each ambassador will go to a different group. Those who stay will be the hosts to two ambassadors from the other groups. You will have 15 minutes to share. Invite the ambassadors to briefly introduce themselves and to share what their group learned. Then the host group shares what it learned.

We'll take a 15-minute break, you'll return to your re-formed group, and we'll repeat the process with different questions.

The final 20 minutes will be spent debriefing the café process in the large group. You will have the opportunity to post your notes on the walls for all to see.

(When it's time to set up the ambassador process, restate the following instructions.)

Now it's time to share what has happened in your groups. I invite two people from each group to stand up to be ambassadors. (Wait until you see people doing so. Encourage them to take the risk of going to another group. Wait until all groups have two people standing.) Each ambassador goes to a different group. In other words, the two ambassadors from each group will not be in the same group. Host groups, raise your hands until you have two ambassadors in your circle. Once you get to your new group, introduce yourselves. Host group, welcome your ambassadors. Then begin by sharing what happened in each of the groups. You have 10 minutes to do this!

You will have 5 minutes to summarize what you learned. You can write on the notecards and place them on the wall boards. Then we'll have a break.

Come back to the re-formed group after the break.

Sample Timeline for a 3-Hour Session

1:30–2:00 P.M. Registration
2:00–2:15 P.M. Welcome and introduction to Interfaith Café
2:15–3:00 P.M. Small group dialogues
3:00–3:05 P.M. Look for themes, patterns, common threads
3:05–3:20 P.M. Ambassadors and hosts

3:20–3:35 P.M. Break
3:35–4:20 P.M. Small group dialogues
4:20–4:25 P.M. Notice themes, patterns, and common threads
4:25–4:40 P.M. Ambassadors and hosts
4:40–5:00 P.M. Reporting to large group

Café Etiquette

Speak from your heart.
    Use "I" statements.
Listen with respect.
    Listen for understanding, not necessarily agreement or belief.
Discover and explore.
    Listen for patterns, themes, new questions.

Guidelines For Café Hosts

The role of the host for the Interfaith Café is to support the conversation, not to lead or manage it. You are holding the space in which the conversation occurs. We offer these suggestions as possible ways to create this support.

1. Invite people to introduce themselves *briefly*: name, where they live, and faith tradition or spiritual path.
2. Review the café etiquette and ask for agreement. If the group has additional ideas to add, make sure that everyone agrees. Mainly we are here to learn more about each other, not to debate positions. Suggest that people listen for patterns or themes in the conversation, rather than rehearsing what they will say.

3. Repeat the question and invite the dialogue. There is no need to call on people. Allow the conversation to emerge. Some groups may want to go around the circle, others may be more comfortable with free-flowing conversation. Let whatever wants to happen, happen. Invite personal experiences and stories.

4. Allow 40 minutes for everyone to speak on the question. Invite someone to be a timer, and give the group a 5-minute warning or whatever time the group would like.

5. The next 5 minutes is an opportunity for the group to notice whether there were any themes, patterns, or threads in the conversation or whether new questions arose.

6. At this point, the café facilitator will invite one or two group members to stand up and become ambassadors; the rest will stay where they are as hosts. As a café host, please stay with your group. The ambassadors will split up and each one will go to a different group. The hosts will welcome the ambassadors to their groups.

7. Take a minute to do brief introductions. Then have each ambassador give a 2–3 minute summary of his or her group's conversation, and one of the hosts will do the same for your group.

8. Spend the last 5 minutes talking about what this was like and what questions or themes emerged from the conversations. Write comments on notes, one per page. Post questions on the wall, flip charts, or wall boards.

9. There is a break for 15 minutes. Return to this re-formed group.

10. Repeat steps 4 through 8.

11. There is a 20-minute debriefing with all groups about the process and about what participants learned.

12. Invite a brief closing ritual for your small group. Acknowledge and thank them for sharing from their hearts.

Sample Questions

How do your religious beliefs influence the way you:
Have fun (entertainment, relaxation)
Choose your friends
Speak (use of jargon and slang)
Work

How do your religious beliefs influence the way you:
Pray
See the world
Make difficult choices

What is the impact of spirituality on your everyday life?

How do I define peace?
What beliefs obstruct the achievement of peace in our world?
How do I apply my faith to peace?
What is my contribution to peace and social concerns?

How can we learn to understand one another better?
What is the most difficult principle in my faith to practice?
How does my faith impact my stance on current affairs?
How does my faith affect my engagement with a secular society?

Notes

1: What Is Listening?

1. Ernest Hemingway, "Monologue to the Maestro: A High Seas Letter," *Esquire,* October 1935. Reprinted in *By-Line: Ernest Hemingway*, edited by William White (New York: Bantam Books, 1967), 190.

2. Paul Hawken, "Listening Could Relieve Strife That Leads to War," *Philadelphia Inquirer,* August 22, 2002.

2: Contemplative Listening

1. Sister Wendy Beckett, *Sister Wendy's Book of Meditations* (New York: DK Publishing, 1998), 20.

2. Meister Eckhart, as quoted in "The Silence of the Soul," by Laurence Freeman, *The Tablet,* May 10, 1997.

3. David Steindl-Rast, *A Listening Heart* (New York: Crossroad, 1999), 66.

4. Mairead Corrigan Maguire, as reprinted in *The Vision of Peace* (Maryknoll, N.Y.: Orbis Books, 1999), vii.

5. Anne Morrow Lindbergh, *Gift from the Sea* (New York: Pantheon Books, 1975), 41, 42.

6. Henri Nouwen, *Reaching Out* (New York: Image Books Doubleday, 1975), 125, 136.

7. Mohandas K. Gandhi, *Young India,* January 23, 1930.

3: Reflective Listening

1. Sue Bender, poster published in 1992 by Portal Publications, Ltd., Corte Madera, Calif.

2. Rainer Maria Rilke, *Letters to a Young Poet* (New York: W. W. Norton, 1954), 34–35.

3. Rachel Naomi Remen, "Just Listen," from *Kitchen Table Wisdom* (New York: Riverhead Books, 1996), 143.

4: Heart Listening

1. Peter Senge, *The Fifth Discipline Fieldbook* (New York: Currency/Doubleday, 1994), 377.

2. Carl Rogers, *A Way of Being* (Boston: Houghton Mifflin, 1980), 143.

3. Rebecca Shafir, *The Zen of Listening* (Wheaton, Ill.: Quest Books, 2000), 117.

4. Thomas Merton, "Hagia Sophia," in *A Thomas Merton Reader,* edited by Thomas P. McDonnell (New York: Doubleday, 1989), 506.

5. Martin Luther King Jr., *Letter from a Birmingham Jail,* April 16, 1963.

6. Mother Teresa, "Women's Voices: Quotations by Women," compiled by Jone Johnson Lewis, The History Net, www.womenshistory.about.com.

7. John S. Dunne, *The Reasons of the Heart* (Notre Dame, Ind.: University of Notre Dame Press, 1978), 39.

5: Opening Space for Listening

1. Margaret J. Wheatley, *Turning to One Another* (San Francisco: Berrett-Koehler Publishers, 2002), 88.

2. Joseph Jaworski, *Synchronicity* (San Francisco: Berrett-Koehler Publishers, 1998), 178.

3. Douglas Steere, *Gleanings: A Random Harvest* (Nashville, Tenn.: Upper Room Books, 1986), 83.

4. Taizé Community, The Value of Silence, www.taize.fr.

5. John G. Neihardt, *Black Elk Speaks: Being the Life Story of a Holy Man of the Oglala Sioux* (1932; Lincoln: University of Nebraska Press, 2000), 150.

6: The Impact of Listening

1. Brenda Ueland, "Tell Me More," *Utne Reader,* November/December 1992, 104.

2. Paul Tillich, as quoted in James B. Simpson, *Simpson's Contemporary Quotations* (Boston: Houghton Mifflin, 1988), 183.

3. Carl Rogers, *Freedom to Learn* (Columbus, Ohio: Charles E. Merrill Publishing, 1969), 225–26.

7: Listening in Groups

1. Rainer Maria Rilke, in a letter written December 27, 1913.

2. David Augsberger, *Caring Enough to Hear and Be Heard* (Ventura, Calif.: Regal Books, 1982), 12.

3. Teilhard de Chardin, as quoted in James B. Simpson, *Simpson's Contemporary Quotations* (Boston: Houghton Mifflin, 1988), 196.

Selected Readings

Albom, Mitch. *Tuesdays with Morrie: An Old Man, a Young Man, and Life's Greatest Lesson.* New York: Doubleday, 1997.

Backman, John. *Why Can't We Talk? Christian Wisdom on Dialogue as a Habit of the Heart.* Woodstock, Vt.: SkyLight Paths, 2013.

Baldwin, Christina. *Calling the Circle: The First and Future Culture.* New York: Bantam Books, 1998.

Barker, Larry, and Kittie Watson. *Listen Up: How to Improve Relationships, Reduce Stress, and Be More Productive by Using the Power of Listening.* New York: St. Martin's Press, 2000.

Beckett, Sister Wendy. *Sister Wendy's Book of Meditations.* New York: DK, 1998.

Bender, Sue. *Everyday Sacred: A Woman's Journey Home.* San Francisco: HarperCollins, 1996.

———. *Plain and Simple: A Journey to the Amish.* San Francisco: HarperCollins, 1991.

Black Elk, as told through John G. Neihardt. *Black Elk Speaks: Being the Life Story of a Holy Man of the Oglala Sioux.* Lincoln: University of Nebraska Press, 2000.

Blanton, Brad. *Radical Honesty: How to Transform Your Life by Telling the Truth.* New York: Dell, 1996.

Bohm, David. *On Dialogue.* New York: Routledge Press, 1996.

Bolen, Jean Shinoda. *The Millionth Circle: How to Change Ourselves and the World—The Essential Guide to Women's Circles.* Berkeley, Calif.: Conari Press, 1999.

Burley-Allen, Madelyn. *Listening: The Forgotten Skill: A Self-Teaching Guide.* New York: John Wiley & Sons, 1995.

Carnes, Robin. *Sacred Circles: A Guide to Creating Your Own Women's Spirituality Group.* San Francisco: HarperCollins, 1998.

Chopra, Deepak. *The Seven Spiritual Laws of Success: A Practical Guide to the Fulfillment of Your Dreams.* San Rafael, Calif.: Amber-Allen, 1995.

Cooper, David A. *A Heart of Stillness: A Complete Guide to Learning the Art of Meditation.* Woodstock, Vt.: SkyLight Paths, 1999.

Eck, Diana L. *Encountering God: A Spiritual Journey from Bozeman to Banaras.* Boston: Beacon Press, 2003.

Ellinor, Linda, and Glenna Gerard. *Dialogue: Rediscover the Transforming Power of Conversation.* New York: John Wiley & Sons, 1998.

Farnham, Suzanne G., Stephanie A. Hull, and R. Taylor McLean. *Grounded in God: Listening Hearts Discernment for Group Deliberations.* Harrisburg, Pa.: Morehouse, 1999.

Farnham, Suzanne G., Joseph P. Gill, R. Taylor McLean, and Susan M. Ward. *Listening Hearts: Discerning Call in Community.* Harrisburg, Pa.: Morehouse, 1991.

Gefen, Nan Fink. *Discovering Jewish Meditation: Instruction & Guidance for Learning an Ancient Spiritual Practice.* 2nd ed. Woodstock, Vt.: Jewish Lights, 2011.

Goldberg, Philip. *Roadsigns: Navigating Your Path to Spiritual Happiness.* Emmaus, Pa.: Rodale Press, 2003.

Harris, Rachel. *20-Minute Retreats: Revive Your Spirit in Just Minutes a Day with Simple Self-Led Exercises.* New York: Owl Books, 2000.

Housden, Roger. *Sacred America: The Emerging Spirit of the People.* New York: Simon & Schuster, 1999.

Isaacs, William. *Dialogue and the Art of Thinking Together: A Pioneering Approach to Communicating in Business and in Life.* New York: Doubleday, 1999.

Jaworski, Joseph. *Synchronicity: The Inner Path of Leadership.* San Francisco: Berrett-Koehler, 1998.

Johnson, Ben Campbell. *Listening for God: Spiritual Directives for Searching Christians.* New York: Paulist Press, 1997.

Kamenetz, Rodger. *The Jew in the Lotus.* San Francisco: HarperCollins, 1994.

Kernion, Anne Kertz. *A Year of Spiritual Companionship: 52 Weeks of Wisdom for a Life of Gratitude, Balance and Happiness.* Woodstock, Vt.: SkyLight Paths, 2016.

Lindahl, Kay. *The Sacred Art of Listening: Forty Reflections for Cultivating a Spiritual Practice.* Woodstock, Vt.: SkyLight Paths, 2002.

Lindbergh, Anne Morrow. *Gift from the Sea.* New York: Pantheon Books, 1983.

Maguire, Mairead Corrigan. *The Vision of Peace: Faith and Hope in Northern Ireland.* Maryknoll, N.Y.: Orbis Books, 1999.

Miller, Rhea Y. *Cloudhand, Clenched Fist: Chaos, Crisis, and the Emergence of Community.* San Diego, Calif.: Innisfree Press, 1996.

Millis, Diane M. *Conversation—The Sacred Art: Practicing Presence in an Age of Distraction.* Woodstock, Vt.: SkyLight Paths, 2013.

————. *Deepening Engagement: Essential Wisdom for Listening and Leading with Purpose, Meaning and Joy.* Woodstock, Vt.: SkyLight Paths, 2015.

Muller, Wayne. *Sabbath: Restoring the Sacred Rhythm of Rest.* New York: Bantam Books, 1999.

Nouwen, Henri J. M. *Reaching Out: The Three Movements of the Spiritual Life.* New York: Image Books, 1986.

Owen, Harrison. *Expanding Our Now: The Story of Open Space Technology.* San Francisco: Berrett-Koehler, 1998.

Pennington, M. Basil, Thomas Keating, and Thomas E. Clarke. *Finding Grace at the Center: The Beginning of Centering Prayer.* 3rd ed. Woodstock, Vt.: SkyLight Paths, 2007.

Quinn, Susan. *The Deepest Spiritual Life: The Art of Combining Personal Spiritual Practice with Religious Community.* Ashland, Ore.: White Cloud Press, 2003.

Remen, Rachel Naomi. *Kitchen Table Wisdom: Stories That Heal.* New York: Riverhead Books, 1996.

Rosenberg, Marshall B. *Nonviolent Communication: A Language of Compassion.* Encinitas, Calif.: PuddleDancer Press, 1999.

Ruiz, Don Miguel. *The Four Agreements: A Toltec Wisdom Book.* San Rafael, Calif.: Amber-Allen, 1997.

Salwak, Dale. *The Wonders of Solitude.* Novato, Calif.: New World Library, 1998.

Schaper, Donna. *Sacred Speech: A Practical Guide for Keeping Spirit in Your Speech.* Woodstock, Vt.: SkyLight Paths, 2003.

Senge, Peter. *The Fifth Discipline: The Art & Practice of the Learning Organization.* New York: Currency/Doubleday, 1994.

Shafir, Rebecca. *The Zen of Listening: Mindful Communication in the Age of Distraction*. Wheaton, Ill.: Quest Books, 2000.

Steindl-Rast, Brother David. *A Listening Heart: The Spirituality of Sacred Sensuousness*. New York: Crossroad, 1999.

Stone, Douglas, Bruce Patton, and Sheila Heen. *Difficult Conversations: How to Discuss What Matters Most*. New York: Viking Penguin, 1999.

Thich Nhat Hanh. *The Miracle of Mindfulness: An Introduction to the Practice of Meditation*. Boston: Beacon Press, 1987.

Walsh, Roger. *Essential Spirituality: The 7 Central Practices to Awaken Heart and Mind*. New York: John Wiley & Sons, 2000.

Wheatley, Margaret J. *Leadership and the New Science: Learning about Organization from an Orderly Universe*. San Francisco: Berrett-Koehler, 1992.

———. *Turning to One Another: Simple Conversations to Restore Hope to the Future*. San Francisco: Berrett-Koehler, 2002.

Wicks, Robert. *Snow Falling on Snow: Themes from the Spiritual Landscape of Robert J. Wicks*. New York: Paulist Press, 2001.

Yankelovich, Daniel. *The Magic of Dialogue: Transforming Conflict into Cooperation*. New York: Touchstone Books, 2001.

Zander, Rosamund Stone, and Benjamin Zander. *The Art of Possibility: Transforming Professional and Personal Life*. New York: Penguin, 2002.

Websites to Explore

Many groups around the world are engaging in small group dialogue and conversations. The following websites provide information and ideas.

www.commonway.org
www.conversationcafe.org
www.conversationmatters.com
www.heartlandcircle.com
www.millionthcircle.org
www.peerspirit.com
www.publicconversations.org
www.theworldcafe.com

There are many interfaith organizations that foster dialogue in their gatherings. I have had personal experience with the following groups:

www.contemplativeoutreach.org
www.masteryfoundation.org
www.nain.org
www.parliamentofreligions.org
www.theforge.org
www.uri.org

ACKNOWLEDGMENTS

Two of the many gifts in my life are that I know I am living a life I love and I know I am doing what I was meant to do. I am profoundly grateful for this knowledge and for these gifts, so my first acknowledgment is to God, Source, Creator, Divine Love. Each day I am inspired by the wonders of creation and awed by the Divine Wisdom that guides my life. Thank you.

My next acknowledgment is to my family. To my parents, Dagney and Tryve; my sister, Joan, and her husband, Jack; my children Andrew and Joan, Wendy, Thomas, Victoria, Laura and Zach, Tony, and Steve and Audra; and my grandchildren Ashley, Tommy, Madeline, Rebecca, Ryan, Kevin, Logan, Kennan, Svea, and Zinnia. You continue to teach me how to listen and your love and support sustain me, especially when I have to be away from home. Thank you for showing me the power and joy of our love for each other.

This book wouldn't have been written without the encouragement of Jon Sweeney and the professional support of Maura Shaw, Emily Wichland, Lauren Seidman, Shelly Angers, Barbara Heise, and the entire team at SkyLight Paths. Thank you.

I am deeply grateful to the hundreds of participants in the workshops, retreats, and presentations I've made over the past several years. You have risked being vulnerable with each other and with me, you have demonstrated the power of listening in the way you responded, and you have taught me how to teach this work. Thank you.

Amy Schnapper, whose artwork illustrates this book, continues to be friend, business partner, and confidante. I am deeply grateful for your ongoing ability to help me see where I'm stuck and to empower me to find solutions so I can move forward again. Thank you.

The following people went above and beyond in providing me with assistance, material for the book, and/or moral support: Bob Anderson, Phil Goldberg, Tony Hotchkiss, Barbara Nixon, M. Basil Pennington, Fred Plumer, and Susan Quinn. Thank you.

All of my interfaith activities and encounters have nurtured and supported me in writing this book. The list would go on for many pages were I to publicly acknowledge each individual and organization. It all started with one dedicated group, the Alliance for Spiritual Community, and I want to acknowledge the current board of directors for all their work and for their constant encouragement: Rick Costa, Frank Hotchkiss, Barbara Grossman, Fran Kieffer, Kathy Sandoval, Jan Schreiber, Melvin Scudder, Khaled Tawfik, Sharon Upp, and Bev Waterman, and past board members Don Barkley, Gloria Fetta, Joe Firoved, Michael Friedman, Stan Grubin, David McClelland, Charmane Riggs, and Ellen Severino. Thank you.

Finally, to my husband, my dear and enthusiastic mate, whose spirit enlivens the world. Thank you for always being there for me and for seeing the light in me when I forget, for assuring me that I can do whatever it is I need to do, and for loving me.